T0209574

IT HAPPENED ONE WEEK IN JERUSALEM

When Christ Was Crucified

GEORGE M. GOODRICH

WESTBOW
PRESS®
A DIVISION OF THOMAS NELSON
& ZONDERVAN

Scripture quotations marked ASV are taken from the American Standard Bible.

WestBow Press books may be ordered through booksellers or by contacting:

WestBow Press
A Division of Thomas Nelson & Zondervan
1663 Liberty Drive
Bloomington, IN 47403
www.westbowpress.com
1 (866) 928-1240

ISBN: 978-1-9736-5268-7 (sc)
ISBN: 978-1-9736-5269-4 (e)

Library of Congress Control Number: 2019901091

Print information available on the last page.

WestBow Press rev. date: 02/19/2019

INTRODUCTION

THE IDEA FOR THIS BOOK really started when I heard a story on the internet concerning Logan and how he had to put down a calf because its mother couldn't provide the necessary nourishment[1]. Logan was just a 10 or 12 year old at the time and the son of a farmer. I don't know if that internet site is still active as you read this, but it was a sad tale from a young son of the farmer and the calf was basically his responsibility. He was a wise young man for his age, however, and reflected on the task as being similar to God having to "put down His son". He made the comment that he couldn't imagine how God felt when His son was put on the cross. Since I have difficulty knowing how God felt as well, I accepted this lack of understanding as a challenge for writing this book. I chose the last days of Jesus here on earth as the inspiration. I wanted to see if I could put this sacrificial act into a perspective that I could understand. Although I didn't use every act, the ones I chose were selected to determine if I could put myself into Jesus' situation and respond as Jesus did or at least respond according to my understanding and interpretation of how Jesus responded.

REFERENCES

1. https://www.youtube.com/watch?v=zCdZwitrNoY

DEDICATION

THIS BOOK IS DEDICATED TO my family: my wife, Sandra, of 56 years (this year 2018), my two sons, Michael and David, my daughter, Adona (Homminga): my grandchildren: Michael Ryan, Arlyn, Corisssa, Rigel, Austin, & Elijah and Aleida; and my great grandchildren, Kent, Chandelier, & Elly; and to the wives and husbands of my children and grandchildren, Tracy, Brien, Allison, and Mariah. By dedicating it to all of them, I am hopeful that they will benefit from the wisdom or lack there of put forth in this effort to relate my feelings and beliefs about who this book is really dedicated to and that would be Jesus, son of God, my savior.

ACKNOWLEDGEMENTS

ALTHOUGH THE THOUGHTS PRESENTED IN this book are my own, I acknowledge that I have had generous help putting the thoughts into words. I especially appreciated the proofing my wife Sandra provided. Equally important were the contributions pastor Keith Foisy of Evergreen Covenant Church in Branch, Michigan. Some individuals like Karla Foisy, and Eric, my physical therapist, also provided input that was very helpful. I thank them all for their patience and understanding and willingness and enthusiasm in their assistance.

The photographs, including the cover photograph of the cross in the sanctuary of Evergreen Covenant Church in Branch, Michigan, are my photographs used with my permission.

ACKNOWLEDGMENTS

ABOUT THE AUTHOR

GEORGE M. GOODRICH IS A graduate Metallurgical Engineer with over 50 years of consulting experience in the world of metallurgical failure analysis and foundry technology, none of which has anything to do with the subject of this book. However, he has put his writing experience from his professional world to use in addressing the issues surrounding Jesus' death and resurrection he has found inspiring all throughout his career. With an active church life serving in various capacities throughout the years as teacher, secretary, treasurer, Board Chairman, lay missionary, and even presenting an occasional Sunday morning message, he has plenty of experience to share on the subject. His first book, <u>Adventures with Apples and Snakes in the Garden of Eden</u> addressed the obedience issue from the beginning. This current endeavor addresses a completely different aspect of obedience, Jesus' death and resurrection!

CONTENTS

PRELUDE

I CAN'T EVEN PRETEND TO imagine what God thinks. However, I can imagine what I think about God and I can give you my thoughts about what I think God imagines with the imagination God has given me.

In this first chapter, Christ is breaking bread with his disciples. Comparing "breaking bread" with Christ's "broken body" requires us to imagine how his broken body was a sacrifice for our broken lives. It might even require us to seriously consider the fact our lives are indeed broken.

FIRST, HE WAS ALIVE

CHAPTER 1
Break THIS Bread!

I know what you say may be true,
But how can you be certain I won't misunderstand you?

"[26] AND AS THEY WERE eating, Jesus took bread, and blessed, and brake it; and he gave to the disciples, and said, Take, eat; this is my body."[1] Symbols, how much more simple can you get than breaking bread. Jesus told his disciples on more than one occasion [2, 3, 4, 5] he had to be judged, punished, and crucified. They obviously did not understand, or, perhaps, chose not to understand. Most likely, they understood, but did not want to accept what they understood. Jesus knew it was time for this nonsense about ignoring the inevitable to end or else all was going to be lost with the efforts he was putting forth. This was the "last supper". It was now or never. The final task was at hand. He needed his disciples to understand.

This was not for larks. Maybe the disciples had been having a good time traveling the countryside with Jesus from Galilee to Jerusalem, but the good times were about to come to an end. This was serious business and the seriousness of the business had to be understood. The time for learning had come to an end. Now was the time for the tests. Jesus had accepted their misunderstanding up to this point, but not anymore. He had patiently taught them; and taught them; and taught them time; and time again. They had spent three years experiencing most unusual interactions with people. Thousands had listened to Jesus. Miracle after miracle had been performed. Yet, the disciples still were so human!

Being understood or more appropriately being misunderstood seems to be universal. Employees misunderstand their bosses and bosses misunderstand their employees; children misunderstand their parents and parents misunderstand their children; wives misunderstand their husbands and husbands misunderstand their wives. Friends misunderstand friends. Enemies misunderstand enemies. Pastors misunderstand parishioners and parishioners misunderstand pastors!

Today's modern communication tool, E-mail, is the worse media for exchanging information without misunderstanding. Repeatedly, in my everyday work effort, misunderstandings between my boss and me occur and have wrecked what could have been an excellent working relationship. The problem is I work remotely to the office and do not have day-to-day contact with my boss except through E-mail. He directs my activity without face-to-face encounters. It is bad enough to communicate effectively with personal interactions, but to have communications remotely means we do not have the benefit of seeing the effect of the communication on the faces of the individual.

The attempts Jesus had at communicating with his disciples had the benefit of face-to-face experience; it had the benefit of visually seeing the outcome; it had the benefit of seeing the teaching is action; and yet, the disciples didn't fully understand the message until after the act Jesus had forecasted. When people make the effort to tell us as directly as possible, we still manage to hear only what we want to hear.

Jesus broke the bread and said "this is my body".[1] From my perspective I can't help but wonder if the disciples really understood what he was trying to tell them even then. His body was about to be broken and they wouldn't be able to put it back together. The bread like his body was broken so they would remember Jesus. The bread was broken so all of us would remember what Jesus allowed his body to go through for us. Not only that but the bread was broken so we would have a symbol to remind us what he had gone through for us.

The problem is the act has such far reaching significance we can't seem to relate it to a single meaning. The sacrifice? What was the sacrifice? The suffering? Why was there a need for suffering? The punishment? Why was there a need for the punishment? And most of all, the death! Why was there a need for his death? These questions and many more go through our minds as we contemplate the significance of this first memorable act at Jesus' last supper. Is it any wonder the disciples had difficulties understanding what Jesus was telling them?

I can imagine the disciples must have sat there with a very perplexing and profound misunderstanding. Broken bread—broken body? How are we supposed to understand this? Yah, sure, now 2000 years later we can at least relate it to Jesus death on the cross, but the reaction of the disciples without the crucifixion must have been one of extreme wonderment. Yet, Jesus chose this symbolism to try and make his point one last time. Jesus was hopeful the disciples would at least put it together the day after tomorrow.

Peter had an inkling about what was going to happen, but even he didn't fully understand. Jesus told him it would take the coming of the dawn and a rooster crowing[6] before he would manage to begin to understand. This was a complicated business and Jesus knew he had to do this awesome task before anyone completely understood. Otherwise, his friends wouldn't let him do it. As the dawning was occurring, these friends still managed to use the wrong weapon and an ear was cut off[7].

Most of my professional life has been spent in the technical world where the communicated word is essential to relating the solution to problems that have been given to me to solve. Being clear and concise is required if you want to avoid spending a great deal of time explaining yourself. Even then, the tiniest misstatement is quite likely to bring a plethora of misjudgments that will tangle your thoughts beyond their original intent. This is especially true if the matter is being litigated. To protect ourselves in this technical world, we add statements to our communications that are designed to alleviate the confusion that can result from the possibility of misinterpretation. Statements such as: stating an opinion to a reasonable degree of engineering certainty; or claiming the right to change our opinion if new information is uncovered. I remember one occasion where I wanted a client to allow us to conduct a certain test so we could be positive about the cause of the failure. The attorney suggested being positive about our certainty might cause the opposing attorney to have grounds for our opinion to be disallowed since "we weren't positive" but only "reasonable".

At times, I find this same aspect bothersome when trying to maintain a reasonable relationship with my wife. When she misstates something, which we all do as we get older, her claim of a reasonable degree of certainty is "you knew what I meant". I am not supposed to make an issue of it if I knew what she meant. Well guess what? Sometimes I know what she means and sometimes I don't. The consequence is I am in trouble the moment I attempt to tell her, I don't understand. I suppose, more importantly, it is the way I tell her I don't understand. I tend to misinterpret the wrongly stated circumstance to the point of ridiculousness and, of course, as intended, she takes issue with the ridiculousness of the misinterpretation.

Even more importantly, I find my inability to communicate bothersome when I try to maintain a relationship with God. Like you I suppose, I am accustomed to using the communication skills God has given me when I associate with other people. However, those same communication skills don't work with God, at least they don't work for me. It seems to be a one-way conversation. I talk to God, but He doesn't respond to me the same way people respond. The feedback I get isn't a spoken word I can hear with the ears He gave me. Rather, the response is in my mind associated with my God given surroundings and my God given abilities. You will note the excessive use of the pronoun "my". It is not hard for me to imagine God around me. However, it is hard for me to imagine God talks to me directly with words and a personal intercession.

It is human nature to not want to be misunderstood. It is weird, though, how we manage to go through our day trying to hide our true feelings and when somebody figures them out, we are upset about that as well.

Sometimes we misinterpret on purpose. I know I like to find out what others are thinking about a particular situation and will, on occasion, switch my argument from one side of the issue to the other without warning and wait for my "opponent" to feel the frustration of not being able to get his point across.

Jesus needed his disciples to understand his mission and if they understood his bread breaking, that was great. However, I think he thought they would have something to put together with the events he knew were about to happen even if they didn't understand at that moment. His body was going to be broken. He was going to suffer. He was going to die. He was going to be sacrificed for the world and the disciples needed to know the meaning of this act thoroughly if they were going to fulfill their part of this story.

In order for the disciples to eat the bread, they needed to break it. In order for Jesus to share his purpose, he had to have us break his body. He saw to it that it was broken and challenges each of us to make the same sacrifice. If you don't stand for something, you stand for nothing, and if you don't stand for something worth giving your life for, you haven't gotten the message yet. Most of us are still accepting the sacrifice and are saying thank you. The grace of God is such that He will allow us to do that. The message of the good news is that we all fail in this regard, but God still loves us. The answer as to why it was necessary for Jesus to be sacrificed is "LOVE"! John 3-16 tells you it is so! I think God knows we understand He wants us to love Him in return to the point we are able to do His will unconditionally, even if it kills us. So why don't we? Can you "break THIS bread"? Jesus did!

QUESTIONS:

Certainly, the disciples had their own notions about why Jesus was in their lives and doing what he did. I think they also managed to let these preconceived notions interfere with their understanding. I also think that each of us has our own preconceived notions about the purpose for God sending his son to show us what God wants us to know.

1. Why do you think the disciples had such a difficult time understanding what Jesus had been telling them about how he would have to be punished and ultimately killed?

2. What aspect of Jesus' broken body is most difficult for you to accept?
3. Can you imagine what it is Jesus knew about humankind that required Him to break his body to save us?
4. When you break bread (or consume the bread element of Communion), what aspects of your broken life are you giving up?
5. Why do you think it is so difficult for you to live your life as if Jesus has atoned for all the sins you have committed?
6. Being misunderstood seems to be a universal problem. Who do you think is mostly to blame for the misunderstanding, you or the person listening to you?
7. Do you think Jesus was difficult for the disciples to understand?
8. Do you think Jesus is still difficult to understand?
9. What is it you have found worth giving up your life?

REFERENCES:

1. Mathew 26:26
2. Mark 8:31 – 33
3. Mark 10:32 – 34
4. Mathew 20:17 – 19
5. Matthew 21:33 – 46
6. Mathew 26:34
7. Mathew 26:51

PRELUDE

IN CHAPTER 2 THE CHALLENGE is to accept Jesus' blood and the wine as a permanent representative of the sacrificial act Jesus committed. Blood is the carrier of life and was considered so holy it was never to be consumed. Yet, Jesus is asking us to drink it in remembrance of Him.

CHAPTER 2
Drink THIS Wine!

The fruit of the vine isn't just wine,
It is the life of a son given for all time.

MATHEW, MARK, AND LUKE ALL say the same thing about the wine in the cup at the last supper [1,2,3]. They say Jesus said it was his blood and it was going to be given to show the commitment between God and His people, a covenant, more specifically, a new covenant that renewed God's commitment to His people. Accepting that commitment from God seems to be relatively easy and for the most part, it can be taken without a whole lot of ceremony. In fact, in some instances, one might feel so blasé about the communion event it might be considered as no big deal. I mean, after all, you just need to accept the cup when it is passed and swallow the offering, right? Once you do, however, if you are like me, you suddenly realize the personal significance of the occasion. God gave up his only begotten son to prove His commitment to me; to prove He loved me despite all I have done! It is impossible for me to drink the communion wine, the blood of Jesus, without thinking about the dedication he had to his purpose! Although the act of drinking the wine and accepting God's commitment seems simple enough, it is impossible for me to perform this communion act without acknowledging the part Christ has played in my life! I haven't ever dared to try and ignore that commitment when I have taken communion. As a matter of fact, there have been more than a few occasions when I just really didn't feel my life was righteous enough to accept that commitment and I took the communion with a great deal of reluctance.

Jesus spent three years teaching he was here to show the Israelites, the chosen people of God, the people God freed from slavery in Egypt, the people who were living in the Promised Land, there was more to the promise than just being their God! Jesus had spent three years teaching he had come to fulfill the LAW, not just show how to live the LAW. He had spent three years teaching the commitment to God was way beyond acts of sacrifice. He had spent three years teaching the love that was involved went way beyond maintaining a nation solely dedicated to His purpose. The time had come to prove beyond a shadow of a doubt, no, I mean way, way, <u>way</u> beyond a shadow of a doubt, that God's love was forever; to prove God's love needed to be spread beyond God's "chosen people"! It isn't difficult to imagine all of us are God's chosen people

Here Jesus was at a supper specifically set aside to celebrate one of the greatest God events in history, God's passing over killing the first born, if there was lamb's blood on the door post[4]. Here he was offering his friends a cup of wine to drink and was setting them up with something new. Were they listening? "A new covenant!" More bloodshed for God's people, blood <u>from</u> the first-born son rather than blood to save the first born! Are you listening, disciples? Blood! Jesus said, "this is <u>my</u> blood"![5] This Passover was Jesus' last supper. He knew it! But his disciples hadn't made the connection yet. It wasn't just a renewal of the long-standing covenant between God and His chosen people, it was a new covenant between God and all His people. His son's blood was going to be shed, not lamb's blood, his son's blood was going to be given so God the father would pass over all people. Saving the first born in Egypt was just an example of what God was capable of saving. Now, he was going to save all people and he was going to make the biggest sacrifice of all, His son!

Reducing this commitment to a personal level causes much consternation for most of us. I can't possibly imagine what God had to do to pull off such a feat! For example, I can't possibly imagine giving

FIRST, HE WAS ALIVE

CHAPTER 3

Take THIS Cup!

When a challenge is presented
Do you wonder if God meant it?

I HAVE ALWAYS WONDERED HOW Jesus felt when the Passover Supper ended. Here he was at a party celebrating an age-old event commemorating the freeing of all Israel from slavery. Yet, he knew this would be his last time to celebrate this event in the traditional manner. He knew he was about to go through an excruciating demise. He knew one of his friends was going to identify him to the Pharisees and they were seeking to humiliate him. He knew the humiliation was going to end with more than ridicule and embarrassment. He knew he was going to be put to death. He knew he needed to pray.

The walk he took to the Garden of Gethsemane from where he had his Passover celebration was probably about a mile through the Kidron Valley. After he arrived at the garden, he was looking for support. He took three of his most trusted friends with him to pray. These friends must have been accustomed to praying, after all, they had been traveling with him for three years. The support went to sleep[1]! No wonder he cried out: *"Abba,* Father," he said, "all things are possible unto thee; remove this cup from me: howbeit not what I will, but what thou wilt."[2]

It is not hard to imagine Jesus is praying about the experience he is about to have. It is not hard to imagine this experience might be more than he can handle. It also isn't hard to imagine the first thing Jesus did once he knew he was about to be subjected to the final judgment of mankind, was pray. It is also not hard to imagine he wanted some trusted friends at his side while he struggled with the meaning of what he was about to experience.

Many of us have struggled with decisions we've had to make. We, too, most likely turn to prayer and look for support from our most trusted friends. It is amazing to me that just like Jesus, the only support that makes sense comes from the Lord. Only one person can make the decision. Only one person can make the commitment that is required. Yes, I agree each person is, to some extent, responsible for others and must consider as much as possible the impact on others his decision will make. Like Eve in the Garden of Eden, the decision will impact the life of many others for eons to come. Hopefully, Jesus did a better job in his garden of Gethsemane than Eve did in Eden.

We all have a purpose. To be certain, discerning that purpose is a challenge. Some of us spend a life time trying to determine just what that purpose is. The problem is we also pray for the cup to be taken from us and have done precisely what Jesus prayed would happen for him but didn't. The cup wasn't taken from him! We may pray about the issue and seek God's direction, but unlike Jesus, we <u>let</u> the cup be taken from us. In fact, I would venture to say most of us virtually ignore what God asks us to do because it is too hard. Jesus didn't, and God didn't intercede. The inevitable was not prolonged as Jesus seemed to be asking. None of his buddies stepped forward and volunteered to take his place either. <u>**No**</u>, they went to sleep!

We look for the outs or even more realistically, we ignore what we are called to do. We pray "show us your will" then we ignore what we see. We pray "thy will be done" then decide what His will is. We don't know how weak we really are. Perhaps it is an innate desire for us to take the straightforward way out! We can't come within a country mile of carrying the load Christ carried for us, yet we can come to his table and drink his blood and eat his body and know he understands, just like he understood exactly what it was God needed him to do. What poor examples of so called Christians we really are! Very few of us have what it takes to be willing to sacrifice ourselves for what we believe. Yet, plenty of God's people have and plenty of God's people will. You only need to look at Memorial Day, or the 4th of July or Veterans Day to see examples! Those people were willing to make the ultimate sacrifice. Can we determine our purpose? Don't ignore the obvious when you look for God's will in your life.

Still, even the example of good Christians willing to "fight" for something as a solder is not representative of what Christ did. Over the years, the message we hear in sermons and in conversations with our pastors[7] teaches us Jesus died on the cross in love for mankind not in protecting mankind from themselves. Solders have weapons to protect themselves. Jesus had weapons too, but his were a different kind, among them being, Love, Faith, Hope. I think we get sidetracked in our thinking with the entertainment we see on television, and in the stories we read, and the news we hear. That sidetrack is the thinking we have power to overcome evil with super hero stuff. My two grandsons exemplified this "sidetrack" during a recent visit when they spent hours in front of the television playing war games with all sorts of different weapons. The news media ignores the fact that lives have been sacrificed in wars for unreasonable endeavors, usually for the longings of someone else and most likely we don't even know who the person is personally. Christ wasn't trying to kill his enemy or even protect his country; it was his love for mankind that was driving his sacrifice. This isn't taking anything away from those who have given their lives for our freedoms, we certainly thank them, and we commemorate their sacrifices, but Jesus' sacrifice isn't comparable to the heroes we recognize in some of our holiday celebrations. The appreciation we have for Jesus's sacrifice is different than the celebrations for our "war heroes" and it should be!

When you have identified a task in need of being done, how do you know the task is what God wants you to do? Here is a test you can apply. If the result of the task glorifies the Creator, it is something God wants you to do. If the result of the task glorifies you, you have forgotten who the real creator is. Like Jesus, prayer puts the task into proper prospective. Jesus understood what needed to be done. Yet, here he was making certain this was exactly what God wanted him to do.

In the end, the decision was his and his alone. His "buddies" went to sleep and were of no value at all. This was between him and God. I can't imagine what was going through his mind. He must have been beside himself with anxiety and frustration and doubt. I can't possibly imagine having God ask me to go through what Jesus went through. That kind of imagination, I don't have.

Yet, here he was praying and knowing the task was at hand. Here he was giving his commitment to God. "nevertheless, not as I will, but as thou wilt.⁴" I can imagine Jesus' "will" was anything but going through with this awesome task. This verse is telling us Jesus admitted he could not do it on his own. I can imagine this is the real story. Adam and Eve had already tried to do it on their own and they couldn't come close to obeying God over an apple let alone over such an impossible task as giving their life up for God.

Abraham was willing to give up his son's life⁵, but no angel came to save Jesus. This time the sacrifice of the son was going to happen. This time he was the lamb that was going to be sacrificed. This time he was the ram with his horns caught in the thicket⁶. This time God needed us to sacrifice a real son, His son. I can't imagine how bad God thinks we really are that He would ask us to sacrifice His son to prove we fear Him⁷. I can't imagine what this is going to prove at all. This is the real problem isn't it! How can we imagine sacrificing God's son is going to prove anything? No, we can't imagine sacrificing God's son will prove anything because Jesus isn't our son, or is he? Maybe this is what Jesus was praying about: taking God seriously! How about the rest of us? Can we take THIS "cup" seriously, seriously enough to stay awake? Seriously enough to actually be willing to give our lives for the purpose of celebrating God? Take THIS cup in deed!

QUESTIONS:

"Taking this cup" references the situation in the garden of Gethsemane where Jesus was asking God in prayer to intercede and I

FIRST, HE WAS ALIVE

CHAPTER 4
Pray in THIS Garden!

Decisions to make
Require faith that won't shake.

JESUS HAD JUST FINISHED CELEBRATING the Passover meal in the "city"[1]. This somber celebration commemorated how God had passed over the Hebrew nation and saved their first born from death. It isn't difficult to imagine how the somber event had left Jesus in want of prayer. Passing over the first born and being the first born himself, he felt a strong need to seek God's input for a task he knew would require his death despite being the first born. No passing over this time! So, he went to a familiar place near the Mount of Olives, the Garden of Gethsemane[2]. Undoubtedly, he was familiar with this place from previous visits. This garden was close to where his friends, Lazarus, Martha, and Mary lived. So even though the bible doesn't tell us he had been there before, in all probability, he knew this garden provided the atmosphere he needed to clear his mind for the task that lay before him. Judas knew where the garden was as well, and obviously, he knew this was where Jesus was going to go[3] after his Passover meal. Yet another betrayal in a Garden where God and man walked together!

This walk to the garden was not a short trip on foot; Gethsemane is located about 1/3 mile west of Jerusalem, but it was across the Kidron valley and the path was steep on both sides of the valley. Yet, Jesus felt compelled to go there. The internet has many maps and photographs to help you appreciate the terrain Jesus had to traverse to get to the garden. Reference 4 has several maps that are helpful.

Just the week before this Passover event, Jesus and his disciple had completed their trek to Jerusalem from Galilee. Jerusalem is located about 70 miles south of Galilee and the trip had taken several days and probably even weeks. All during the trip Jesus had been talking about what was going to happen to him once they arrived in Jerusalem[5]. Now the time had come for these foretold events to take place. Jesus needed this time in the Gethsemane because he knew the final chapter was at hand. It is impossible for me to imagine how Jesus who knew what was about to transpire was just going to let it happen. How could he? What an awesome challenge! So, he went to his safe place, Gethsemane. It is no wonder he sought a place to pray. The events that took place in the garden that evening, the praying, the disciples need for sleep[6], disciples obviously hadn't been listening to Jesus' preaching and had not taken him seriously[7]. In fact, they had argued about who would be first with him. Even in the garden, they didn't pray with him. What did the disciple do? They went to sleep!

There is no doubt Jesus was agonizing about what was going to happen. Considering the prayers he was offering, and the intensity of his praying[8], one has to wonder if he was looking for a different way to fulfill his destiny. He was definitely seeking God's help for the upcoming task. There is no doubt about him asking for God's strength to go through with this task[9]. His words, "My Father, if it is not possible for this cup to be taken away unless I drink it, may your will be done"[10] even have us wondering about his willingness to go through with the task. Of course, it has us wondering! I don't believe any of us would be willing to do this task without some divine intervention! In fact, I would venture to guess none of us would be willing to step into Jesus' sandals at this point even with divine intervention. So, it really isn't difficult for any of us to imagine some sort of hesitation on the part of Jesus to go through with this awesome task.

Because we are Monday morning quarterbacking these events, we can see and understand the significance of the events that are about to happen. However, at that moment, it is extremely difficult for us to imagine what was going through Jesus' mind. He knew what he had to do yet he knew his disciples were not ready to understand the significance of the acts that were about to transpire. They wanted to sleep!

The Garden was Jesus' refuge. It was his place to commune with God. I believe we all can agree, Jesus needed to have a one-on-one conversation with God. His disciples didn't seem to have this need, but Jesus did. The disciples had listened, but had they heard? Not only did Jesus need this time to pray, he believed his disciples needed it as well. He asked them to pray with him[11]. He had already told them just a few hours before that he was going to be betrayed[12]. What did his disciples think he was talking about? It isn't difficult to imagine the disciples really didn't want to understand what Jesus was talking about. I don't think any of us under the same circumstances would own up to what they had been told and what they really understood. They may have known Jesus' death was eminent and they may not have understood why, but they knew no matter what, God was part of whatever was going to happen.

I believe the praying Jesus was doing was for all of us to understand his death was a sacrifice. Up until his praying in the garden, he hadn't managed to even convince his disciples he was going to be killed as a sacrifice. He may have convinced them he was going to be killed, but I don't think they were anywhere close to understanding his death was a sacrifice for all of mankind. The disciples knew Jesus had a unique relationship with God, but the son of God? I believe they were still struggling with this concept. Remember at this time in history, God required his chosen people to sacrifice at an alter to atone for their sins. Jesus had just told the disciples a new covenant was in the making[13]. The atonement that was about to take place was a totally new concept, a significantly new way to be at one with God. How could they (or us) possibly understand the significance of this if they (or us) didn't accept he was the son of God? So now after this Passover proclamation and the betrayal he had told them about, Jesus had the difficult task of accepting now was the time. He chose his Gethsemane, his refuge, his place for being alone with God. He was praying God would make this event as meaningful as the scriptures had foretold. Jesus was asking for the rest of us to understand he was the way to eternal life. Gethsemane was a place where they pressed olives to make oil. It is fitting that Jesus chose this garden to "press his relationship" with God. Jesus' final act of obedience was the culmination of a life-long endeavor to be obedient to God. This "even unto death" was just part of that life-long relationship with His Father. Death on the cross was just part of that obedience, an important part, yes, but still just one part! Most of us take the death on the cross as the sacrifice, but the bigger picture is it was the final act of obedience as a human being which atones for our sins.

As I sit here and write this, it is still difficult for me to understand let alone imagine how Jesus' death is a sacrifice for all of the world's sins. To be totally honest, it is really most difficult for me to imagine he is the sacrifice for my sins let alone for all of the world's sins. The garden of Gethsemane was not the last place Jesus prayed for us, but it was the last place he went willingly to do that praying. Jesus needed this refuge. He knew he had to have this alone time with God. All of us need this at oneness with God from time to time. We may not call the place we go Gethsemane, but we all have our Gethsemane of some sort. My wife uses her gardening for that purpose. I use my alone time in the mornings for that time. I also use my alone time in the morning to get my thoughts organized so I don't start my day on a "chippy" note. Sometimes, my alone time is during hunting in my tree stand; sometimes it is in my boat fishing. None-the-less, I don't consider myself unique and honestly believe we all need our "garden time" with God.

Earlier in my life when I needed to make an important decision about the direction of my career and for my family, it was easy for me to empathize with Jesus' need to commune with God about decisions that needed to be made. Not only the empathy, but the aloneness at making the decision also impacted me. Jesus wanted his disciples to help him with the challenge, but no, they went to sleep. No one can make the decision for us on any matter God wants us to fulfil. God expects us to move off the fence and to use the talents He gave us to accomplish His goals. Too often we know what we are being asked to do and almost equally all too often we pray that He find some other way to accomplish the task. If we could only see forward! However, looking back, it is not hard to imagine the tasks He has asked me to do were way easier than what I could imagine. Fortunately, Jesus can also look back at the task God was asking him to do and see what has been accomplished. Two thousand years later, here we are thanking God for sending His son to sacrifice himself for our sins. We may not understand, but we sure spend a lot of our alone time in our gardens thanking God for being included in that sacrifice! When do you pray in THIS garden?

QUESTIONS:

It isn't difficult to imagine the necessity for Jesus to find a place to talk with his father. He had some life changing decisions to make. He chose to make those decisions in one of his favorite places. He also asked some of his trusted friends to join him in his moment of decision.

1. What are some of your favorite place to go when you want to communicate with God?
2. What aspects of Jesus' life to come do you think he was praying about when he asked God to "take this cup from me"?
3. When you read about the disciples falling asleep after being asked to pray with Jesus, what were your thoughts?
4. What do you think was going through Judas' mind with his betrayal at this moment?
5. Celebration of the Passover was eons old! What parallels do you see between the first Passover event and this sacrificial event that was about to happen?
6. Why do you think we struggle with the concept that Jesus gave his life as a sacrifice for our sins?
7. Do you think that Jesus was praying about the decision to follow God's wishes or do you think he was praying for something else? If "something else", what do you think is was?

8. What kind of events in your lifetime can you equate to this occasion where Jesus took time before a very important event to talk it over with God?

9. When you are praying in "your garden", do you wish for someone to be praying with you?

REFERENCES:

1. Mathew 26:18
2. Mathew 26:36
3. Mathew 26: 47
4. The Jeremiah Study, <u>Worthy</u> 2013
5. Mathew 20:17-19
6. Mathew 26:40
7. Mathew 20:20-28
8. Luke 22:44
9. Luke 22:43
10. Mathew 26:42
11. Mathew 26:41
12. Mathew 26:21
13. Mathew 26:26-29

PRELUDE

ALL OF US HAVE BEEN subjected to accusations we know are false. Maybe they are from misunderstandings; maybe they are from people with ill intent; maybe they are accurate but misinterpreted; maybe they are just plane false! It could be they are true as well! No matter what the source or the cause, we almost always react. Our reactions telegraph the nature of who we are. The trouble is our reactions are also frequently misinterpreted and we would have been better off to not say anything and not react at all!

CHAPTER 5
Answer THESE Charges!

No words can describe how you feel
When your integrity is challenged without appeal

FROM MATTHEW 26:62, "AND THE high priest stood up, and said unto him, Answerest thou nothing? what is it which these witness against thee?" I can imagine Jesus just letting the high priest and his cohorts stumble through the fictitious allegations trying to find someone or something they could use to justify the actions they intended. What I have a difficulty imagining is just letting these priests have their own way. Jesus basically said if it wasn't meant to happen, it wasn't going to happen[1] (my interpretation!). Most of us would have a tough time simply letting events like his happen to us. For some reason, we are just not mentally built that way.

My first job after I graduated from Michigan Tech was with a major manufacturer in their research laboratories. I had a master's degree in metallurgical engineering and was anxious to contribute what I could with my ideas to the success of my employer. It was a great place for a young engineer with a desire to share his God given talents. This particular industry had quite a reputation for the extremes in their business activity.

While I was employed with this manufacturer, the economy was in a down turn and pay raises for salaried employees were limited to annual cost of living adjustments just so the professional staff could keep up with what the union employees were earning. A time came, however, when merit raises were once again being considered. Since I had been working there for about eight years and had not received a merit raise for approximately the last 5 of those years due to the economy, I thought it was time for a merit raise.

I approached my supervisor and inquired about my eligibility for a merit raise. He informed me that merit raises were only being considered for those employees with potential. I then inquired how they measured potential and was informed potential was measured by degrees and I only had a master's degree.

You need to know I really liked working there. This was my idea of how to use my God given talents. I was having difficulty with the politics, but the work was exactly what I had envisioned when I graduated. However, at that moment, the moment I was hoping my employer would have the same vision for my future as I did, it was obvious they had different feelings about my continued employment than I did. On the spot, I told my supervisor I desired to take him up on an offer he had made to me during one of my previous reviews. He had told me if I ever became tired of working there he would help me find a position within the corporation that would utilize my capabilities. When I finished reminding him of his offer, I informed him that just a moment ago, I had become tired of working there. I left for another job within 2 weeks and it wasn't a job in that corporation.

This story regarding my first job may not be anywhere near close to what Jesus was experiencing, but the story does reflect how most of us would react to a situation that was not in keeping with what we might perceive as our due. It was hard for me to imagine how a place I liked to work didn't have the same feelings as I did about me working there. Apparently, Jesus had similar feelings about his stay on earth. Jesus couldn't imagine how the Sanhedrin were not able to understand why God had sent him in the first place. Add to this the fact the Sanhedrin was trying to find someone to say something against him. After all, being as close to God as they said they were ought to have allowed them to understand the significance of Jesus' life on earth. I know when my integrity is challenged, it is very hard for me to accept what I am being accused of doing. It isn't hard for me to imagine Jesus couldn't believe what he was hearing. What was wrong with these people? They were so far from the truth of the matter, there was no way for them to develop an understanding that would make a difference. I can imagine Jesus was really taken aback at the difference between the reasons he was on earth and the accusations the Sanhedrin had manufactured for their charges. His only reaction was to let them proceed. He knew they were not going to listen to him anyway!

From our perspective, Jesus' apparent way of life was being threatened. He had been wandering the countryside for three years preaching and teaching, healing and otherwise marking his existence with commendable acts that went way beyond normal ways of life. These acts certainly established that he was no ordinary person. They established that somehow, he had a direct link with God the creator. Yet, here he was standing accused facing ridiculous charges and he was not behaving in a manner his disciples were accustomed. If his disciples didn't understand this behavior, is it any wonder we have difficulty understanding this behavior as well?

My supervisor was not accustomed to me behaving in the manner I behaved either. I think he may have underestimated me. The priests had underestimated Jesus as well. They thought Jesus would react and behave with denial and give them even more reason to justify the actions they intended to take. My supervisor undoubtedly thought I was more than willing to accept whatever he was going to give me because he believed my dedication to my employer was more deeply embedded than it was. The priest thought Jesus was dedicated to making them look foolish and were expecting a much different reaction than they were receiving.

The time had come for me to move beyond this first position. Research is for people with fresh and innovative ideas and for people with the most up to date technology. This manufacturer was exploiting the new minds as much as it could. They would not have fired me. I could have continued doing what I was doing, but my value to them was considerably less than a fresh PhD engineer right out of college. It was time for me to move on and it was time for Jesus to move on as well. Jesus said it best, "Neither do people pour new wine into old wineskins."² He had fulfilled all the requirements his ministry had set out to accomplish up to this point. Now it was time to fulfill the next step and he was moving ahead with God's plan for his life.

This matter of Jesus standing there accepting the accusations without a reaction wasn't just an issue of being accused without cause. In my mind, it was an issue of submitting to evil. I apologize to those of you who I might be offending with this out of the ordinary view of Jesus, but this is not how I perceived Jesus would behave in a situation where his life would be at stake especially in front of such evil and in face of such outlandish accusations especially from the very people who had created the conditions that had caused God's disappointment. Up until now in the Jesus story, Jesus was teaching and healing and doing many wondrous things. For him to just stand there and take these accusations without reacting to the charges doesn't seem to be in character. Then again, maybe he wasn't submitting to evil but instead was not going to overcome evil with evil! Now that would be in His character!

Accepting the notion that I submit to the desire of my employer to not give me a merit raise because according to their measuring stick I had no potential was just not in my nature. For Jesus to submit to the evil that was being used to accuse him of doing wrong is not in my character either. I can't imagine how this idol of mine could just stand there and accept these fabricated accusations. For him to just stand there and take these accusations just do not match up with my expectations of how God wants us to behave when we are face to face with evil.

After writing this and having it reviewed by a pastor I know, I realized with his input that maybe I have mixed idol with hero! Maybe I have "idolized Jesus"! Maybe if I had considered him my hero instead of making him my idol I wouldn't have had to apologize before I wrote the paragraph about him just standing there seemingly to take the insults without reaction. Making Jesus an idol would account for my inability to rationalize His reactions. Making Him my hero would justify my reaction to His response. A hero might not fight evil with evil, but an idol might!

Yet here he was, facing Caiaphas who was demanding that Jesus tell him if he was the son of God: "I charge you under oath by thee living God: Tell us if you are the Messiah, the Son of God."[3] My savior could have ended all of this if at that moment, he demonstrated as he had done many times before that he was in fact the son of God. Jesus' answer was: "Jesus saith unto him, Thou hast said: nevertheless I say unto you, Henceforth ye shall see the Son of man sitting at the right hand of Power, and coming on the clouds of heaven."[4]. Was this all the action Jesus was going to take? Where was the fire he had just a few days before when he threw the moneychangers out of the temple? If anything needed throwing out at that moment, it was Caiaphas and his cronies. Instead, they spit on Jesus and struck him.[5, 6]

I can't imagine Jesus being short of words. He had been preaching for three years convincing others that living for God was the most important thing one could do. If he could convince the Sanhedrin, he most certainly would have convinced the most influential body of people. Here was his big chance, the opportunity to achieve his goal of convincing the Jewish people worshipping God meant much more than achieving personal advantage. The charges being leveled against him was exactly what he wanted to achieve, and they were using his objectives against him. I can imagine Jesus' frustration. I can imagine him wondering why they didn't understand. I can imagine him saying you'll never understand this matter until you see the real power sitting at the right hand of God. I hope that is not what it takes to convince me!!!!! THESE charges were nothing in comparison to the real issue, being God's person for real. Being like Jesus who was all these things is the real issue!

QUESTIONS:

Being subjected to an inquisition of the magnitude that Jesus faced must have sent his mind reeling in a multitude of directions. Although I have been subjected to situations where I was questioned for hours in depositions, I was required to answer. Jesus wasn't! But, I have not been accused of something I did not do. I don't know how I would handle that. Being required to give a testimony is bad enough!

1. What do you think was going through Jesus' mind when the high priest was questioning him?
2. When you had an occasion to be accused of something you didn't do or an occasion where what you did was right in your mind but not in the minds of other people, how did you react and what were the consequences?
3. What aspect of your life would you NOT change no matter what?
4. Dedication is an important aspect of your character. Have you developed a statement or organized your thoughts to the point that you can describe what you have dedicated your life to achieve?
5. How do you think the preaching and miracles Jesus had done were linked to demonstrate what he had dedicated his life to achieve?
6. How do you imagine Jesus should have reacted to Caiaphas' accusations?
7. What do you think was going through Caiaphas' mind as he questioned Jesus?
8. When you encountered people who misunderstood what you were intending to accomplish with your actions, what did you do?
9. Have you ever altered your path as the consequence of being wrongly accused or encountered an impossible situation? What has been the consequences?

REFERENCES:

1. John 19:11
2. Mathew 9:17
3. Mathew 26:62
4. Mathew 26:64
5. Mathew 26:67
6. Mark 14:65

PRELUDE

ALL OF US FROM TIME to time find ourselves in positions where others think we shouldn't be. The antics these people go through to discredit us usually brings out our worst nature and desire for retaliation. How we respond is a credit to our principles and what we believe is the difference between right and wrong. In most instances, however, our reactions (at least my reactions) precede justified responses and reflect insufficient forethought until we decide that the situation is way beyond our abilities to judge the correct reaction accurately in the available time. When we do judge the situation accurately, we are elated because the "police" we were wondering about became apparent (like where are the cops when you need one?).

CHAPTER 6

Wear THIS Crown!

When people don't understand,
They can't wait to ridicule and command!

THE SOLDIERS WOVE THORN BUSHES into a crown and placed it on his head and gave him a scepter made of reeds mocking his claims about the Kingdom of God. It was their understanding that he claimed to be king of the Jews[1, 2]. I don't understand where this "King of the Jews" claim originated. None-the-less, the soldiers were acting in accordance with their understanding no matter if it was real or imagined. What Jesus actually did, what he actually said, and what people understood him to claim certainly has caused much consternation for centuries. Visualizing this misunderstanding should not be difficult. All we need to do is look at the last two thousand years of divisions in the "church" Jesus started. Nothing in any of the Gospels state Jesus claimed to be King of the Jews. His kingdom claims were all associated with the Kingdom of God, not the Jews. In fact, when Pilot asked Jesus specifically if he was king of the Jews, his first response was:

"Sayest thou this of thyself, or did others tell it thee concerning me?"[3]

His second response was:

"My kingdom is not of this world: if my kingdom were of this world, then would my [servants fight, that

I should not be delivered to the Jews: but now is my kingdom not from hence."[4]

Interpretation! Interpretation! Interpretation!

Pilot "washed his hands" of the matter[5] and ordered Jesus to be flogged[6]. This was just an example of the many degradations that the captives (the Israelites) had to endure as a result of the Roman Empire's need to keep their captives at bay. The Jews were desperately looking for relief from just such cruelties. Jesus was offering an alternative, but he was up against a culture where a select few had an advantage in this cruel system. These select few didn't want to lose this advantage.

This desire to retain their advantage had consequences! The Jewish leaders and others in authority, like Pilot, "consequently misunderstood" Jesus. Perhaps this "misunderstanding" was intentional. However, the soldiers who were given the task of dishing out the punishment were apparently "allowed" to believe whatever they wanted to believe if it provided the impetus to make their captives suffer.

Nevertheless, Jesus was a danger to the existence these Jewish leaders enjoyed. Additionally, the Roman Governors didn't want problems that would require them to take drastic measures. Doing away with a single individual was a lot easier than fighting an entire nation. These few Jewish leaders were determined to have the Roman Governors rid themselves of Jesus because of the challenge Jesus created to the existence these leaders enjoyed. Their existence was limited considering their captive circumstances, but it was better than they could imagine if the followers of Jesus were to succeed with their claim that Jesus would relieve them of the pain and suffering they obviously were experiencing under Roman rule. More importantly, these leaders didn't want the status quo upset by someone they couldn't control.

They needed the Romans to take care of this problem, so they could go on with what little advantage they had gained. They didn't need any radical new ideas casting suspicion on their motives. They needed the Romans to have a reason to get rid of this challenge to their existence.

Placing the crown on Jesus' head and giving him a scepter was the very response these disgruntled Jewish religious leaders were trying to achieve. They wanted the Romans to mock and ridicule Jesus so their value could be put into a more favorable light with the Romans and with the Jewish people. Jesus, as a target, definitely had the high visibility they needed in order to achieve this goal and the time was just right. These Jewish religious leaders needed to distract the Romans in order to continue with their deception of the Jewish people. This mocking and ridiculing raised the importance of Jesus to an even higher level than existed before he was arrested. Think about it from this direction: if Jesus had been "a nobody", if he had been without any significant following, if his claim of being the son of God had no validity, the Romans wouldn't have wasted their time with him. However, because Jesus <u>was</u> who <u>he</u> said <u>he</u> was (not who others said he was) these mocking acts have held a high degree of significance for more than two millennia. These acts may have momentarily served the Jewish leader's purposes. However, God had a grander plan. He has always wanted us to be part of a Kingdom that is "not of this earth". His plan has always been for us to be part of a Kingdom He guides with his son seated at His right hand. The Kingdom of right relationships, as some people have called it. The mocking and ridicule of Jesus has had considerable notoriety over the millennia. In fact, this mocking and ridicule notoriety has gone further to accomplish God's purpose than the Jewish leaders of the time have accomplished to achieve God's purpose.

The Jews wanted a King that would save them from the cruelty of the Roman Empire. They indeed had a king, King Herod Antipas.[7] However, he was King because of his political ties. He was King because of the allegiances with the Roman Empire his father had made. His father was known as Herod the Great. He was "The Great" because of his great building skills, not because of his popularity with the Jewish people. Herod the Great built the port at Caesarea, many theaters, fortresses, aqueducts, and other public buildings throughout Judea. The Jewish people especially recognized Herod The Great for expanding their temple in Jerusalem. This expansion was intended to gain the favor of the Jewish people. However, that favor was not achieved to any great extent. Although King Herod Antipas' father had achieved[8] these great building tasks, he did not enjoy any degree of popularity with the Jewish people. Herod was also an Idumean and not fully Jewish, which was a huge problem for the Jews. Herod Antipas had even worse relations with the Jewish people than his father. Is it any wonder the Jewish people were anxiously awaiting a messiah? The Romans suppressed them, yes, but even worse, their own religious leaders and their Kings suppressed them as well. The Jewish religious leaders during the time of Jesus could not afford to have their status challenged.

Being used for political schemes has not stopped with this crown of thorns and the ridicule Jesus went through. Many of us go through these trials and tribulations nearly every day. Several instances stand out in my life. I remember one instance involving a Planning Commission for a small village. Two prominent individuals in the village had a piece of property located on Main Street they wanted to sell to a bank for a branch outlet. The area was zoned "residential" and required rezoning to "commercial" to achieve the proposed use. The Planning Commission was not in favor of singling out one parcel of land for a commercial use in the middle of a beautiful residential area. This was precisely why the village had formed a Planning Commission and charged them with developing a zoning ordinance to foster growth in a manner that would preserve the quaintness of the village. They had just completed a study and had put forth a new zoning ordinance the Village Council had approved after three years of work. The Planning Commission was not willing to have the results of their efforts jeopardized so soon after they had completed the work. As far as they were concerned, the Village Council and the community were in agreement with their plan. However, the local newspaper promoted the new proposed use. These influential individuals used their positions to force the issue in their favor with threats to parents with children in the school system. I know that one of those threats still aggravates one of the Planning Commissioners since it involved his son who was in kindergarten at the time. The threat was to keep the son in kindergarten if he didn't vote in favor of their desired use. This one influential individual was using a "crown of thorns" and was placing it on the planning commissioner's head and the ridicule he was taking in the newspaper as Chair of the Planning Commission were not pleasant. He resigned rather than give in to their demands and subject his young family to the occurring ridicule. The schemes these individuals used worked, and the town now has a bank branch in the middle of a residential neighborhood on Main Street. I visited the village a good number of years after the event. The town had grown where the planning commission envisioned the growth, but they also have a bank branch right where the influential individuals wanted it, in the middle of a predominantly residential area. I don't think either of the two individuals are there any longer. Who knows what would have happened if the Planning Commissioner had managed to withstand the ridicule and the crown of thorns. I hope his son would have graduated from kindergarten by now.

In my career, I have had five different employers. I know from experience in those jobs that employees can be the subject of ridicule co-workers will put forth to the boss. When an employee feels threatened because a relatively new employee is promoted to a position parallel to an employee with more time on the job strange, undesirable events can happen. These "strange" events become even more strange if the boss is going to be retiring in a few years and competition occurs for the boss' position when it becomes available. In one instance I recall, these strange events resulted in one employee being promoted while the other employee left the organization. The first competitor went on to gain the executive position he was seeking. Ultimately, the organization lost it prestige, lost its tax status, lost its treasurer (who was jailed for embezzlement), and the competitor retired. Before he retired, however, the Board of Directors of the organization placed an overseer in a position of authority over his executive position and basically rescued the organization from bankruptcy. These events are interesting to me because 35 years later, the individual that had left the organization went on to receive a prestigious award from the organization for his dedication to the industry and was asked to give a keynote address at one of the organization's annual meetings.

Wear this crown indeed! Jesus went on to lead a whole new endeavor to bring people back to God. The religious leaders of the time have left no lasting impact on society since Jesus' time. Indeed, everything has changed. The Temple is no longer central to Judaism. The Pharisees, however, were the beginning of a new tradition which would become the Rabbinic movement. This is the movement that Judaism is based on today. This movement gave Judaism a future even without a Temple, which no one would have been able to imagime as a long-term solution.

The Roman Empire put down a rebellion in Judea around 70AD and destroyed the temple.[9] Judea hasn't been the same since. They were exiled, subjected to slavery, scattered amongst many nations, and basically have been non-existent as a nation until 2000 years later when their country was reestablished. The Roman Empire became extinct and God's Jewish people are still waiting for their messiah while the rest of the world has moved forward with the good news that God's love is for all. The good news is to gain God's love, all one needs to do is just ask for it and accept Jesus as his or her personal savior. I can't imagine what God felt when He saw His son being ridiculed, mocked, and whipped. On the other hand, the meaning of the crown has gone way beyond what the soldier intended. God let his son go through this ridicule for all of us. The challenge becomes one that requires us to be willing to go through ridicule for Him. Wear THIS crown! Jesus did!

QUESTIONS:

No doubt, you have been subjected to a humiliating experience. I don't know anybody who has not. The extent of the humiliation may not have been anywhere close to what Jesus experienced, but the way in which you reacted has probably nagged you for a long time.

1. How do you interpret the word "kingdom" and how does your interpretation relate to your desire to be part of what you imagine?

2. As a citizen of a democratic country, what "kingdoms" do you see existing today?

3. Think about what drives you to do what you do and define the "crown" that would typify the epitome of that endeavor.

4. What do you think the Jewish leaders were afraid of as it related to Jesus existence?

5. Why do you think Pilot didn't want to have anything to do with what the Jewish leaders wanted?

6. If Pilot thought Jesus was innocent of any wrong doing, why do you think he allowed his soldiers to punish Jesus?

7. What political scheming have you been subjected to?

8. What endeavors have you seen fall apart as the result of political scheming?

9. What "crown" do you see others seeking that you don't believe is worth the effort?

REFERENCES:

1. Mark 15:18
2. Mathew 27:29
3. John 18:34
4. John 18:36
5. Mathew 27:24
6. Mathew 27:26
7. absoluteastronomy.com/topics/**Herod_Antipas**
8. Herod the Great – Britannica Online Encyclopedia
9. "The Romans Destroy the Temple at Jerusalem, 70 AD," EyeWitness to History, www.eyewitnesstohistory.com (2005).

PRELUDE

WE RARELY THINK ABOUT HOW our everyday existence can be offensive to God. How we conduct our lives, our interactions, our exchanges, our manipulations, our simple tasks, are all important to God even though we may not think about them with Him in mind. If we did, I submit to you that these everyday experiences would take on a unique perspective and even a unique meaning. For example, in a recent bible study session, I learned the difference between an "it" and a "thou". When we treat others as an "it", they become a means to accomplish <u>our</u> objectives. When we treat others as a "thou", they become an integral part of our lives and a realization that we are all part of God's creation with God's objectives in mind. The "it" portion is offensive to God and is part of the cross that we must bear to seek forgiveness through the load that Jesus carried for us.

CHAPTER 7
Carry THIS Cross!

I can't imagine what Jesus thought
As he carried the cross mankind had brought.

I HAVE WALKED THE VIA Dolorosa (the Way of Grief or Way of Suffering) in Jerusalem. The literature has many maps to show where this route exists. Reference 1 is one such example. It is a narrow set of streets paved with cobble stones and definitely not on level ground. From what I understand, five streets make up the Via Dolorosa. Three of these streets are within the original walls of the city at the time of Jesus and two are outside of those original city walls. Today, all these streets are within the existing city walls. The contour of this path is very steep in many places both up hill and down. The cobble stones are rough and consist of many varied sizes making walking very tenuous and unstable. The route is very difficult to walk under any circumstance (unless you have the conditioning of a 25-year-old or better). The current route of the Via Dolorosa was established in the 1800's and is intended to represent the path Jesus walked carrying his cross from where he was whipped, beaten, ridiculed, and scourged to the garbage dump where he was hung at that cross. I have included a few photographs of the Via Dolorosa taken during my trip to Israel in 2003 at the end of this chapter.

Today, the streets are lined with small shops selling souvenirs, clothing, food, jewelry, and many other items people sell to make a living. I suspect many of the items have the same life sustaining capability now that they had in the time of Jesus. Stores are stores and they are there to sell what people will pay for. Some of these items sold in these stores are essential for living, but others are truly tourist orientated. (Tourism is the largest industry in Jerusalem today, but in the time of Jesus, the Israelites were required to attend religious events at least 4 times a year, so I suspect many "tourist items" were sold in Jesus's day as well.) The people doing the selling also live in accommodations that are part of the structures along these streets. The appearance of the city along the Via Dolorosa is representative of how Jerusalem appears within the current walls and probably is representative of how Jerusalem appeared in the time of Jesus. The differences between today and Jesus' time most likely would be in the commodities being sold, but the contour, uneven surfaces, and narrowness most likely are representative of what Jesus experienced. In addition, however, the Via Dolorosa also has churches and worship centers marking the route at various sites where Jesus reportedly performed some act while carrying the cross. Some of these acts are noted in the Gospels and some are not. Obviously, these churches and commemorative sites were not present at the time of Jesus. Jerusalem has grown way beyond those original city walls and the walls themselves have changed significantly since the time of Jesus. All the Via Dolorosa today is within the current city walls including the Holy Sepulcher. The Holy Sepulcher is a church built on the site where the crucifixion of Jesus reportedly took place. The garbage dump where the crucifixion occurred was originally outside the city walls, but today, that portion of Jerusalem is within the city walls. Jerusalem outside of the city wall has an appearance today typical of any modern-day city anywhere in the world with automobile, bus, and truck traffic along with the assorted traffic lights, parks, malls, restaurants, museums, and other businesses.

The special sites along the route Jesus walked carrying the cross are known as the "stations of the cross". There are 14 stations all totaled. These stations were established in the 15th century to commemorate the struggle Jesus endured on his way to be crucified. Nine of these stations are actually on the Via Dolorosa. The remaining five stations are in the

Holy Sepulcher. The first two sites at the beginning of the Via Dolorosa represent the location where Jesus was condemned and scourged. The remaining seven stations along the route represent specific events that occurred while Jesus carried the cross.

It is not difficult to imagine the struggle Jesus had carrying the cross. In fact, three of the stations represent sites where Jesus reportedly fell under its load. The bible tells us the load was so heavy the solders ultimately conscripted Simon of Cyrene to carry the cross for Jesus[2]. Even so, scripture also leads us to believe the load the cross represents is more than just the load gravity creates[3].

Walking the Via Dolorosa is considered a pilgrimage and many people do the walk to experience what Jesus experienced. I admit the experience is very emotional and filled with remorse. It is not hard to imagine the anguish Jesus experienced considering all the stops along the way and the different sites commemorating the event. The emotions of walking the Via Dolorosa are the result of realizing none of us can meet the challenge Jesus issued to pick up our cross and follow him. Oh, we follow him all right, and most of us wish we were capable of picking up our cross and walking in his footsteps, but the fact remains none of us has the ability to carry that cross. None of us!

Experiencing that emotional challenge made me wonder why God required Jesus to carry that load. It is difficult for me to think that someone else had to carry my load. I am a very independent person brought up using my own abilities and essentially caring for myself. Oh, I had a roof over my head and food in front of me on my table, but if I was going "to make anything of myself", it was up to me to find the way. The consequence was I gained a great deal of independence and accomplished much in my life because of that independence. It is not normal for me to rely on others to do what I see needs to be done. Even the people who have worked for me and those I have paid to work for me do not seem to be able to carry the loads I envision being required to accomplish the tasks as I see them. That is the problem isn't it? We are all so independent the only path we see is the one we can follow. We trend to ignore the paths where we need help.

In Exodus 20, God laid out the ground rules for us to follow as His children[4]. When we don't follow these rules, we find ourselves separated from God and to correct our relationship with Him, we must make sacrifices. Starting with Exodus 21 and progressing through Exodus 23:13, God set out the consequences for not following the "ground rules". Many of these consequences are "death". We must pay a price to demonstrate when we know our relationship with God has been compromised. This "price" constitutes a "load" we must carry, a sacrifice, until our relationship with God has been "made right". A better way of stating this load carrying necessity is to say we need to atone for our transgressions. These loads were not meant to be easy to carry. God wanted us to pay a huge price for our disobedience, so we would understand the necessity to be obedient. God wants us to want to be obedient and will go to great extremes to teach us the only way to be with Him is to be obedient to Him. These loads were meant to teach us lessons about living in a manner reflecting our obedience to God. It is not hard to imagine in some instances, the load was death. Sometimes we are so bad, death is the only way to make it right with God! You might remember, God told us about death in Genesis, only it was much simpler: if we disobey, we die[6], period.

Jesus walked that path carrying our load. That cross wasn't his load, it was our load for not obeying God with all our heart, all our mind, all our strength, and all our soul. We should have been carrying it, not Jesus. What is really very difficult for me to imagine is we are not capable of carrying that load. We are not able to carry his cross. Jesus willingly died for our disobedience. The most difficult aspect about this cross is we all know he carried our load for us. It is impossible for me to imagine someone else was willing to carry my load! The fact of the matter is he made our load his load. It was the only way he could convince us our sins are offensive to God. He spent three years telling us and showing us and teaching us that our ways, all our ways, are not God's ways. Even when we think we are right with God, the very thought puts us in the wrong because of our self-righteous attitude about being right with God. It is very difficult for me to imagine someone else is willing to carry my load, especially this load. Yet, here

Jesus is doing that very act. Is it any wonder he struggled with this load? My portion is heavy enough let alone everyone else's portion too.

Obedience is ultimately for our benefit, not God's. Our disobedience is what has created the load that is too heavy for us to carry, namely human suffering and brokenness. Jesus took our suffering upon himself. He chose to suffer with us, that we might live in freedom with him. He identifies with us so that we might come to identify with him. I'm not sure that God is offended by our sin as much as he suffers because those he loves are suffering. He enters our suffering and identifies with us so that we might see the great extent of his love and be moved to identify with him.

The question comes down to why Jesus was willing to carry a load that was not his. Although my imagination may not be capable of understanding what ever possessed Jesus to perform this act, I have come to understand God's grace is involved and there is nothing I can do to make up for this act except to accept it with thanks giving. This understanding comes from John 3:16. ("For God so loved the world, that He gave His one and only Son, that whosoever believeth in him shall not perish, but have eternal life.") John 3:17-18 adds even more understanding. ("For God sent not the Son into the world to judge the world; but that the world should be saved through him. [18] He that believeth on him is not judged: he that believeth not hath been judged already, because he hath not believed on the name of the only begotten Son of God.") The price for love is way beyond any understanding I can possibly imagine.

Although God's love is beyond my understanding, the act of sacrificing His only son for me so I can be at one with Him congers up other aspects in my imagination. The price for the act may be beyond my understanding, but the value of Jesus' act as it relates to my existence in God's creation, my existence with God, and my existence with others in God's creation must take on a meaning that becomes a driving force in my life. I must admit, this driving force is not to become Christ like. I am convinced I can not be like Christ. However, I can learn how to develop a life style that is in the spirit of Christ. After all, Jesus did say he would send his spirit to be with us[7] to help us learn all things and remember all Jesus said and did. I suppose this means maybe, just maybe, we ought to pay attention to the load Jesus carried for us. This may be difficult, but think about it from this standpoint: what is the best thing that can happen if we do and if we do not? Better yet, what is the worst thing that can happen if we do and if we do not? Carry THIS cross, if we can!

QUESTIONS:

When we think about Jesus carrying his cross to Calvary and compare it to the loads we carry and how we try to get out of carrying those loads, it is difficult to imagine that someone else has carried our loads for us. Do we connive, do we squiggle, do we justify, do we try to pass the load to someone else, do we blame others? Comparing what we do to what Jesus does is something we really need to spend some time thinking about.

1. What does your imagination conger up when you think about Jesus carrying his cross after being whipped and scourged?
2. What do you think is going through Jesus' mind as he is burdened with the load of carrying the cross?
3. What goes through your mind when you consider the challenge to take up your cross and follow Christ?
4. Jesus needed help carrying his cross, what help do you need to carry the load you have been given?
5. Are you so independent that you don't think you need any help?
6. Why do you think God made Jesus carry this cross?
7. Do you believe that Jesus' cross atoned for what mistakes (sins) you have committed?
8. What does it mean for you to become Christ like?
9. Does the fact that Jesus allowed himself to carry the cross make a difference in your relationship with God?

REFERENCES:

1. https://i2.wp.com/www.seetheholyland.net/wp-content/
   uploads/Via-Dolorosa3.
2. Mark 15:21, Mathew 27:32
3. Mark 8:34; Mathew 10:38 and 16:24
4. Exodus 20:3-17
5. Exodus 21 – 23
6. Genesis 2:17
7. John 15:26

Station III Via Dolorosa (Photo By George Goodrich)

Station V Via Dolorosa (Photo By George Goodrich)

Station IX Via Dolorosa (Photo By George Goodrich)

PRELUDE

CHAPTER 8 MAY NOT STATE it explicitly, but the crux of the cross is about faith. Jesus had enough faith to believe that he had accomplished what God had sent him to accomplish even though he was only ministering for three years. It may seem that He abandoned us and left us to our sinful existence, but, Jesus took it upon Himself to deliver us from our sin despite the fact we don't know how to do it ourselves. Jesus showed us how the Holy Spirit is an integral part of our relationship with God and with our interactions with others. Jesus showed us how to pay attention to the Holy Spirit in such a way that we haven't forgotten the lesson 2000 years later.

THEN HE DIED

CHAPTER 8

Why Have You ABANDONED Me?

How strange it is when we are suffering,
Only then we think of God to provide the buffering.

FROM MARK 15:34 (ASV), "AND at the ninth hour Jesus cried with a loud voice, Eloi, Eloi, lama sabachthani? which is, being interpreted, My God, my God, why hast thou forsaken me?" These words are also part of the first verse in Psalm 22. The rest of the verse in Psalm 22 reads "*Why art thou so* far from helping me, *and from* the words of my groaning?" The second verse in Psalm 22 continues the lament. "²O my God, I cry in the daytime, but thou answerest not; And in the night season, and am not silent." Some say Jesus experienced this abandonment at that moment as he took on the load of humankind's sins[1]. If that is the case, it is easy to imagine Jesus' feeling of abandonment. It must have been crushing. Up until this point in Jesus' life, he had not personally experienced sin. And now there wasn't much life as we know it left for him to experience. No wonder Jesus was expressing his anguish at what he thought was divine abandonment: all our sins piled on him all at once. He literally was experiencing what we should experience during our final judgement. I would say he had every right to ask God why he was being abandoned.

I know this concept is extremely difficult to understand. Sin for us is so common place we don't even know how far away from God we really are. In fact, sin is so common place we don't even consider where we are going in that final judgement. This must really be a disappointment to God; having sin be so common place we accept its presence in our lives without a second thought. Jesus was not accustomed to being so far away from his father and he definitely was not accustomed to being in the throes of this judgement. I can't imagine being so close to God I wouldn't recognize sin or think about what I would have to experience in my final days. What a disheartening thought! It would be a completely different world wouldn't it, if we were able to only experience God's love and not the consequence of sin. I suppose it is possible to imagine living without sin, but this imaginary living definitely is pure imaginary.

I especially like the notion of living in a world without the sins of others. After all, I know others live in a world without my sins. Ya, Right!!!! My sins aren't that bad and certainly you can imagine living in a world without experiencing my selfishness, or my "hooray for me and forget about your needs" attitude, etc. especially since I really don't have much of that attitude nor any of those sins. Ya, Right, again!!!! Sin is so common place for all of us that we go through every day with the sins we commit and think nothing of it. Sin is so common place I'll bet none of us hardly ever asks for forgiveness on a yearly basis let alone a daily basis. Oh, maybe we "ask" for forgiveness when we repeat the Lord's Prayer, but that is so generic we really don't ever stop to specify any particular sin. Some of us might think about specific sins when we take communion.

The Catholic faith requires parishioners to confess their sins to the priests. For us Protestants, we sought the right to go directly to the Lord with our confessions without any intermediary except Christ. If all of us, both Catholics and Protestants, did make more effort to confess our sins, maybe we would be able to better relate to the anguish Jesus was feeling when he experienced God's abandonment as he took on the sins of the world in his last "alive" moments.

Abandonment in many instances is self-imposed as well. From a personal standpoint, I don't mind being abandoned especially when I am going about committing my sins. The last thing I want is to have God looking over my shoulder in my most vulnerable moments which, of course, is while I am sinning. The problem is we know God is there anyway. The real problem is we are not fooling anybody! We are not fooling the people we are sinning against; we are not fooling ourselves; and definitely, we are not fooling God!

Recently, I was reading Jeremiah's Lamentations and they especially caused me to think about the driving force of sin. God told Jerusalem its punishment was complete, and He would not send Jerusalem back into captivity again[2].

God never really abandons us. He does want us to respond with His spirit, however. This issue requires considerable thought. Let me share mine: there is a spirit within us that drives us to be the sort of person we are. I believe for most of us, that spirit drives us to be moral. The drive for morality is there, but so is the drive for the immoral aspects, depravity. Yes, I know there are people who have a spirit that takes advantage of this moral driving spirit and I know there are people who have a purely evil spirit and are driven to live on the morality of others. I also know there are many people who have spirits in between and try to live morally but can't help taking advantage of the giving spirit living in most of us. When the spirit within us experiences the Holy Spirit, our morality becomes holy or at the very least our spirit experiences moments that reflect the attributes of the Holy Spirit, too bad these moments for most of us are short lived and we resort to our selfish selves. Most importantly, when we allow the Holy Spirit to drive us, we become the people of God. Paul said it best in Galatians[3]:

> [19]Now the works of the flesh are manifest, which are *these*: fornication, uncleanness, lasciviousness, [20] idolatry, sorcery, enmities, strife, jealousies, wraths, factions, divisions, parties [21] envyings, drunkenness, revellings, and such like; of which I forewarn you, even as I did forewarn you, that they who practise such

things shall not inherit the kingdom of God. ²² But
the fruit of the Spirit is love, joy, peace, longsuffering,
kindness, goodness, faithfulness, ²³ meekness, self-
control; against such there is no law.

Jesus promised he would send a helper and that helper is the Spirit
of truth.[4] We also know this advocate as the "Holy Spirit".[5] Maybe it
is about time we "took advantage" of the Helper known as the Spirit
of truth rather than taking advantage of each other. After all, can't
you imagine how love, joy, peace, for bearance, kindness, goodness,
faithfulness, gentleness, and self-control might contribute to an
existence that is beneficial to all who you encounter including yourself?

At this most vulnerable near-death moment, Jesus was showing us
the Holy Spirit can be called upon to ease the suffering. The anguish
of these last moments as he was about to descend into "the lower
earthly regions"[6] and "preach to the spirits in prison"[7] or was in fact
experiencing our judgement as he took on our sins, was causing him to
call upon God for relief. In this aspect, he is no different than the rest
of us. Most of us don't think about God until we encounter a moment
we can't handle alone. Even then I submit it takes a unique person to
call upon the Holy Spirit for relief. Instead, we rely on the independence
we have developed over a lifetime of living in the world where we were
born. We are taught from the moment we come into this world to be
dependent and to seek independence. We are initially dependent on
our mothers for sustenance and as soon as we are able, we are taught
to independently feed ourselves and take care of our bodily needs.
This independence, out of necessity, separates us from our parents.
As life progresses, the feeling of independence also separates us from
the love of God and requires us to be "born again" in-order-to become
dependent on God.

Jesus was so dependent on God, he couldn't stand the sin and
had to ask the Holy Spirit for relief. Our anguish is just the opposite.
We can't stand the unconditional love and so we seek relief with sin!
Ug! What a dreary, dreadful thought! But yet, here we are putting
others down because they have offended us in some way; or looking

for entertainment in places where entertainment is less than what God would consider acceptable; or we conger up motives to justify why we treat others with disdain, or we just simply trash the world around us forsaking the greatness of God's creation. I could go on and on, but I am certain you get the picture.

This living independence is why it is difficult for us to give ourselves totally to God. We can't imagine leaving the challenges of our existence to the point of being totally dependent on God for everything. Even though Jesus showed us how, this state of dependence is hard to imagine. It is not a wonder we feel God has abandoned us. We have developed such a keen sense of independence God's presence is mostly unrecognized. God's presence is only considered when we acknowledge our sin has caused us to find ourselves so deep in trouble that we have developed vernacular phases to express the trouble we are in. Yet, we go looking for His support. For those who are not accustomed to these vernacular phrases, basically they mean we have gotten ourselves so deep into sin we can't see any way out. Because we have done it to ourselves, we definitely do not consider God as a first responder and as the sole provider of relief.

I am certain most of us feel there are times when we think God has abandoned us. It isn't hard to imagine Jesus feeling the same way at this particular time. After all, he is just moments away from death. As much as we would like to think he is divine, we often forget about his human nature and he is about to experience death.

I used to think none of us would naturally look forward to this final event, to this last act as a human being, to this "there is no tomorrow" occasion, but recently I have experienced a close relative giving up on a wonderful life. This relative had managed to reach the ripe old age of 90 and was thoroughly enjoying the lives of others who were influential in her affairs. Only, two short months later she found out she had cirrhosis of the liver and pancreatic cancer. This was quite confounding since most of us associate these issues with those who enjoy alcoholic beverages to excess. This was also perplexing because she had never, to my knowledge, even taken a sip of an alcoholic beverage. Once the diagnosis was made known to her, she essentially crawled into a hole and stopped eating and drinking, waiting for the end to come. It is hard for me to imagine wanting to die, but then again, I have never been challenged with the formidable task of trying to overcome something so negative at such a late stage in life.

This act has caused me to wonder why Jesus chose to allow this inevitable death event to take place after only three years of trying to convince mankind a better way existed. I know he had considerable opposition, but the Gospels don't give me cause to believe what he was accomplishing was not making an impact. The Gospels do not give me any clues about any experiences I could possibly imagine in his three-year ministry that would cause him to give up on the life the Creator had given him. By contrast, my 90-year-old relative knew what was about to be experienced. Based on the knowledge of what cancer had done to other family members, the excruciating degradation giving up on life was the only option.

I have seen others in my life do the same and have heard them say on more than one occasion the impending death was something they individually needed to face on a one to one basis with the Creator. However, in all those instances, the individual had definitely arrived at a situation where the only relief they knew was to be brought home to the Lord. When the "end" came, I really don't believe they felt abandoned. My guess is they felt relieved.

I guess that is the point isn't it! After 33 years of life and three years of ministering, Jesus felt his state of existence was so hopeless the only way to make it right was to finish what God had asked him to do without any further delay. Just look at what he had accomplished. Look at all the "thank you(s)" he received for the miracles he did! Perhaps the best example is where he healed 10 lepers and only one came back[8] to say thank you and he wasn't even a Jew! Sort of like thinking we deserve to be healed without giving God the glory for the ability to do the healing. I can imagine what Jesus thought at that moment! Is it any wonder he chose the cross after such a short time of trying to demonstrate that God the creator was Creator of all.

God isn't keeping a secret from us! He hasn't ABANDONED us! So, don't ABABDON Him! It may seem that Jesus gave up on us, but, in reality, his faith in God and his faith in his purpose is an example of how God considers us to be worthy of His love despite what we do to ourselves!

QUESTIONS:

I can imagine that we all wish God wasn't so near at times, only because we have done something that we know He wouldn't approve. The issue is who has abandoned who. "Fessing" up to our wrongs is a good start to realizing how important it is to have the Holy Spirit in our lives.

1. What do you think it was like for Jesus to experience all of mankind's sins all at once?
2. Have you ever had the feeling that you were abandoned? What went through your mind?
3. What does the notion that "sin is so common with us that we really don't know how far away from God we really are" cause you to think about?
4. Most of us God fearing people don't think about the sins we are committing. If you stop to think about it, what sin(s) would you confess out loud right now?
5. What part of the spirit that drives you do you see as being driven by the Holy Spirit?
6. During your normal routine day, what would cause you to stop and think about God?
7. What justification do you use for those rare time you have mistreated your fellow human beings?
8. How far away do you think you are from God?
9. What is it about Jesus' sacrifice that convinces you that your sins have been forgiven?

REFERENCES:

1. Mark Roberts, Senior Advisor and Theologian-in-Residence for Foundations for Laity Renewal, September 2, 2008 <u>Daily Reflections</u>, "Why Have You Abandoned Me"
2. Lamentations 4:22
3. Galatians 5:19-23
4. John 14: 16-18
5. John 14:26
6. Ephesians 4:9
7. 1 Peter 3:19
8. Luke 17:14-16

PRELUDE

ONE OF GOD'S FIRST ACTS when Jesus was dyeing was to turn out the lights, Luke 23:44—45! He brought Jesus in to existence to be the light to the world, John 1:4-5 and what did we do with that light? We crucified it. I think God wanted to show us at that moment what it would be like to undo what he created first, light, Genesis 1:3. What does it take for us to see what God wants from us? Isn't light enough? Turning out the light in Jesus' time meant total darkness. We have it made with all the artificial light we enjoy. Maybe that is it: our light is artificial! What about our obedience? Is it artificial as well?

CHAPTER 9

Only THREE Hours of Darkness?

When Eve's eyes were opened, what did she see?
I'll bet it wasn't eternity!

FROM LUKE 23:44—45 "AND IT was now about the sixth hour, and a darkness came over the whole land until the ninth hour, ⁴⁵ the sun's light failing: and the veil of the temple was rent in the midst." I can imagine at that moment, God was showing his creation just how much He was disappointed with what they had done. What I can't imagine is why it was only three hours! It just seems to me God being God and Jesus being His son "with you I am well pleased"[1]; there should have been a whole lot of commotion expressing how disappointed He was. Cutting off the light for three hours, just doesn't seem to me to be enough of a response considering how God had reacted to His disappointments in the past. After all, over the millennium He had done much worse when He was angry starting with Eve, and Adam, and the snake[2]. Just look at what He did to the Egyptian's first born[3] or to the Israelites when they escaped from Egypt making them wonder in the desert for 40 years[4];

Creating darkness was something He may have done before, I don't really remember. However, darkness existed from the beginning as far as I can determine. It was light He had created with His second creation act[5], not darkness and now He was turning it off. When He created the light, He declared it was good[6]! Now He was sending a different message, a message of extreme disappointment and who can blame Him. Up until this point, He had given humankind all of His creation and they had done nothing but make a mess of it using it to their advantage without regard for the true value of His creation. And as promised[7], He lived amongst us to show His creation how to live with what He had given them. He lived among us as His son. Now, His human creation had destroyed His son! How much worse could it get?

On the other hand, God being omniscient, He had knowledge of a different purpose for this event that mankind didn't have. He knew He was going to raise His son from death in three days. He knew a secret that had not yet come to pass. He knew He intended to cheat the devil from the devil's ultimate weapon, death. He knew the devil had ruled the earth with this weapon since the time of Eve. Fear of death just as God had promised Adam with His "but of the tree of the knowledge of good and evil, thou shalt not eat of it: for in the day that thou eatest thereof thou shalt surely die."[8] statement. Yes, God knew it would take this ultimate sacrifice of His son to bring about the transition He sought. Remember, He originally had what He wanted with Adam and Eve. At least He had what He wanted until Adam and Eve took their apple break! The fact He planned His son's sacrifice still didn't stop Him from letting His creation know He was not going to just let His son be crucified without consequences.

At this point, what our concept of who or what "God" is becomes a limiting factor. Most of us measure the reactions of others based on what we know and what we would do, and because we have limited experience compared to God, we think about this unseemly act of crucifying God's son and consider what God would do based on what we would do if this was our son. If we were God, what would we do to mankind if mankind were to kill our son? The first thing He did was take away the light, at least the biblical account in Luke 23:44-45 would have us believe God took this action! This is a substantial difference from Jesus being the light of men shinning in the darkness[9]. A few other events occurred which we will discuss at length in other chapters but cutting off the light was the first thing He did. What's more, He shut the light off for only three hours! I can imagine with what God is capable of doing He would want to do a whole lot more than just cut off the light for three hours. On the other hand, I am not able to shut off the light like God can!

Only three hours! I still have difficulty understanding this limited act. With what God is capable of doing, being the creator He is, it would seem to me He would choose to show how disappointed He was that His son was crucified with a measure that is a little more extreme than just three hours of darkness. Yet, the fact of the matter is cutting off the light was the first thing God did and here I am still trying to figure out why. Another fact of the matter is we are still here! Although we can't imagine why! I can imagine with the crucifixion of His son, God would react with a vengeance that would terminate all existence. Because we were created in His image and because we have a revenge-oriented mindset, we think God's "mindset" is towards revenge as well. But it wasn't!

From the very beginning, God's intent was for us, His mankind creation, to have an intimate relationship with Him. He has spent thousands of years trying to determine how to give us both freedom of choice and a desire to have an intimate relationship with Him.

God knows until we want to have that relationship, it simply is not going to happen. He spent those thousands of years teaching His chosen people how to experience that intimate relationship. What thanks did He get? He gave them lessons on how to redeem themselves with sacrifices, how to atone for their sins, and how to live cleanly[10]. They repaid Him with misbehavior and defiance. They flaunted His advice over and over again and even killed His messengers. He reprimanded the chosen people beyond what most of us would have tolerated and still He called these people His chosen people. And now they have really done it, they crucified His son! I can't imagine how much more God could take from this thankless lot!

Since that most humiliating experience, He has spent another two thousand years waiting for the meaning of this last sacrifice to sink in. The fortunate part is He is still waiting. He hasn't terminated anything, yet. Oh, I know, many have died and none of us is going to finish this life alive. But that is the way it has always been. Several thousand years ago His human creation lived many hundreds of years, just ask Methuselah[11]. Yet, He couldn't stand the thought of His defiant creatures living forever, so He limited His mankind creation to 120 years[12]! His desire is to get rid of the defiance! His desire is to have His humankind creatures live eternally with Him because they want to, not because He says so! His desire is to somehow show us it is to our advantage to live the life He has given us His way, giving Him the glory. However, being the Creator He is is, He wants that relationship to be without the evil that was learned with the "apple". He knows the evil is there, but He only wants the Good to prevail in His kingdom. He wants our relationship with Him to be only with obedience. No disobedience allowed. Obedience says, "love one another"! Disobedience is self-centered gripping at the expense of another.

I can't imagine my life without having some type of controversy, and I especially can't imagine my life without being dependent on my talents. So, this sacrifice of His son is supposed to cause us to <u>want</u> to be in the right relationship with Him. Before the crucifixion, God had set up measures to provide for sacrifices to atone for every kind of sin one could imagine[13]. More importantly, He had selected a people, the Israelites, to show the rest of creation how to accomplish atonement. He had tried many ways to convince His chosen people to live their life so He could accept them into His Kingdom. Starting with Adam and Eve[14], cleansing with the flood[15], establishing the 10 Commandments[16], devising numerous ways for clean living[17], living through various judges, profits, and kings, and even exile to Babylon[18]. Still, mankind and God were not at one!

The fact of the matter is we were created in God's image, not the other way around. Still, we conduct our lives as if God were created in our image!

It takes darkness for us to see the light!

QUESTIONS:

After all the lessons mankind has received over the eons, it is difficult for me to understand how we can manage to live without at least mentally accepting that where we live was created and that it took a creator to accomplish the creation. I don't believe creation just happened because the circumstances existed to allow creation to happen. I have been led to understand that proof exists mathematically that supposedly our existence and where we exist could statistically happen from random events, but I still wonder where the tools for the mathematical derivation were created.

1. Why do you think we (mankind) need to be taught over and over how to relate to God in a meaningful manner?

2. What is it about our sense of independence that causes us to think we have everything under control until we don't?

3. What is your preferred way of learning, being taught and then experience what you were taught or being put into a situation where you must learn or else?

4. Have you ever had an "Aha! Moment" where you suddenly understood something that you had not understood before? What was it?

5. If light was created, what is darkness? (I know this is a question without an answer, but, take a moment and think about what people would see if we didn't have light pollution.)

6. What kinds of things can you think of that distract from having a right relationship with a friend or a spouse?

7. If you had to sacrifice something to make matters right with a friend or a spouse, what would it be?

8. What kinds of things can you think of that distracts from having a right relationship with God?

9. What do you think you need to sacrifice to make matters right between you and God?

REFERENCES:

1. Mark 1:11
2. Genesis 3:14 – 19
3. Exodus 12:29
4. Numbers 14:34
5. Genesis 1:3
6. Genesis 1:4
7. Zechariah 2:10
8. Genesis 2: 17
9. John 1:4-5
10. Exodus 20 – 23
11. Genesis 5:27
12. Genesis 6:3
13. Leviticus 1:1 – 7:27
14. Genesis 2:3 – 2:22
15. Genesis 6:9 – 8:5
16. Exodus 20:3 – 17
17. Leviticus
18. 2 Chronicles 36:20

PRELUDE

WHAT IS IT SEPARATING YOU from God? I think our imagination generates all kinds of separation issues, and I also think the separation is of our own making. The Jews in Jesus' time had a curtain separating them from where they believed God resided with the Arc of the Covenant. In Chapter 10 we explore how God tore that curtain when Jesus died and eliminated the separation between us and God.

CHAPTER 10
Tear THIS Curtain!

How can we be close to God
Without having heard His nod?[a]

From Matthew 27:51 "And behold, the veil of the temple was rent in two from the top to the bottom; and the earth did quake; and the rocks were rent." The curtain (veil) in the temple tearing from top to bottom was the second God created event that occurred when Jesus died. The account of this event in Luke[1] also gives us the impression that it was part of God's reaction to Jesus' death, just like the three hours of darkness.

Traditionally, Christians believe the tearing of the Temple curtain is a symbol of God's desire to have a one on one relationship with His humankind creation rather than mankind having limited access to God through a priest intermediary. Before tearing the curtain, unless you were a priest and specifically a High Priest from the Levite tribe of the Hebrew nation, you could not go into the "Holy of Holies"[2] (behind the curtain) to directly communicate with God[3]. Even then, you could only go once a year[4]. Apparently, God was sending another message to His chosen people: they had not performed the desired function He had set out for them in accordance with what He had in mind. It was His designated priests who had instigated the death of His

---

[a] Communications! My wife has remarked, on occasion, about not hearing my "nod" when asked if I wanted ice cream or something else.

son, so I can imagine He was sending them a specific message. Two thousand years later we are still trying to understand the meaning of that message!!!! Who can talk with God directly and who can't? Who needs an intermediary and who doesn't?

The "curtain" has a significant meaning in our everyday lives as well. Curtains keep others from viewing what goes on "behind" them. They are used in windows to prevent others from seeing into the room or to keep out light or to keep out heat (or cold). Curtains are used to separate the audience from the actors and stage hands for events like changing scenes. Curtains were used in my house when I was a youngster to separate my "bedroom" from the dining room. Some curtains are see-through so the danger of running into someone unexpectedly is eliminated. These curtains, for example, might be used to keep the cold out of storage area or just the opposite, keep the cold in a heavily used cold storage area. When we think of a curtain, it is a flimsy membrane intended to separate us from some issue others have deemed inappropriate for us to experience. In these instances, it isn't difficult to move the separation aside and experience what is on the other side. The most important aspect is the curtain is intended to separate a person from what is on the other side.

This separation can cause difficulties. If what is on the other side isn't known, imaginary "goings on" can develop. Our minds can come up with all kinds of bad (and sometimes good) situations taking place where we can't see.

One interesting aspect of the "curtain" is it is mostly viewed as a one-way separation. Can you imagine viewing the separation from the opposite direction? There is an old saying about the walls we build. I don't remember where it came from, but the saying is; "the same walls we build to keep others out, keep us in." The curtain in the temple was intended to separate God's people from the "Arc of the Covenant", or from God Himself. I don't think many of us would consider that God used the curtain to separate Himself from us. On the other hand, it isn't hard to imagine God might not want to see what His mankind creatures are doing to His creation. Perhaps the "tearing" of the curtain could also mean God was removing the obstacles that separated Him from us, rather than removing the obstacle that separated us from Him. It is just like us to only view this event one way, our way. When we try to view the event from God's perspective, a whole different meaning becomes attached to the situation. God wants a relationship with His human creatures and is willing to do anything, including allowing His mankind creatures to kill His only begotten son so His mankind creatures would believe He wants an eternal relationship to be established.

The curtain in the temple did indeed separate God from His chosen people or at least that is how the Jews traditional accepted the purpose of the curtain from the time of Moses[5]. In those early days, a curtain was also used to cover the Arc of the Covenant before it was moved[6]. The power of the Arc was understood to the point no one could touch the Arc or even look at the Arc without fear of death[7]. The Hebrew people were afraid of what would happen if the separation was breached and rightfully so since their experience with encounters between humans and the Arc of the Covenant "on the other side" had caused deaths in the past[8].

It isn't difficult to imagine tearing the curtain was intended to indicate what had separated man from God previously was no longer applicable. Since this curtain tearing occurred during Jesus' death, the event has been interpreted as God's desire for a one on one relationship with his humankind creation. One other aspect, we don't have to extend our imagination too far to wonder if the curtain tearing might mean God doesn't want anything more to do with His humankind creation, His human creatures, who crucified His son. Could the curtain tearing be because we humans with our sinful nature have selfish objectives His son was exposing? Still, His human creatures have a spiritual nature that recognizes the wrong they committed and seek a way to resolve the separation from God. I can imagine how humankind can view the torn curtain is a sign of God's willingness to accept a one on one relationship to make matters right between Himself and His human creation. My imagination cannot resolve this matter, but that is where my faith intercedes. I must believe what John tells me; God's love prevails and because of His son, eternal life is available[9]. One interpretation I have heard but don't remember from where is "God has left the building!" In other words, God left Judaism and the religious system.

I can imagine God not wanting anything more to do with His human creation after what we did to His son! That isn't hard at all to understand being the human that I am. All things considered, given the difference between God's intent and my intent, God's motives are on a much higher plateau than mine. Therefore, my imagination is probably misdirected, again! After all, Jesus just finished telling his followers a new covenant now existed. He said it during his last supper[10] and he had said it during previous discussions with those that were considered teachers of the religious law[11]. In fact, as far as Jesus was concerned, this was the new commandment for all of those who believed there were "no other Gods before Me"[12].

Unfortunately, curtains still exist between humankind and God. These curtains no longer are present because of God's commands, however. The curtains I see have been created by humankind to separate what we want God to see from what we don't want God to see. The separation is manmade not God made. We are the ones preventing God from having the relationship He wants.

How foolish we are to think we can hide behind a curtain. This seems to be an age-old story. The Psalmist said it as well: "Wither shall I go from your Spirit?"[13] God's omnipresence precludes any ability on our part to hide behind any facsimile of a curtain. Now it is our turn to tear the curtains. It is our turn to destroy the barriers that separate us from God. He destroyed all the ones He created when He allowed His Son to be sacrificed for the wrong doings we commit. The curtain of guilt; the curtain of sin; the curtain of self-reliance; the curtain of "me first"; the curtain of glory; the curtain of importance; and many many other curtains; they all separate us from the love of God! How foolish we are indeed! Yes, Lord, tear THIS curtain!

QUESTIONS:

Curtains can serve a useful purpose and those purposes are usually easily recognized. That purpose is usually "separation". However, separation also exists without curtains. A torn curtain would normally require fixing.

1. Did the torn curtain in the temple need to be fixed? How do you think the "fix" would look?
2. Have you ever been separated from someone and wondered why the separation existed? Did you make the separation or did the other person?
3. What separates you from God?
4. How do you overcome your separation with God?
5. What is it you know about God that leads you to know that no separation exists between you and Him?
6. What can you imagine exists in your relationship with God that might interfere with His ability to communicate with you?
7. What is it you don't want God to see about your life?
8. Is there anywhere you can go to be away from God?
9. How would your life change if you realized that nothing separates you from what God sees?

REFERENCES:

1. Luke 23:44-46
2. Exodus 26:33
3. Exodus 28:43
4. Hebrew 9:7
5. Exodus 40:33
6. Numbers 4:5
7. Numbers 4:20
8. 2 Samuel 6:6 – 7
9. John 3:16

10. Matthew 26:27 – 28; Mark 14:23 – 24; Luke 22:21;
11. Mark 12:29 – 31; Matthew 22:34 – 40
12. Exodus 20:3
13. Psalm 139:7

PRELUDE

EARTH QUAKES! THE ONLY EARTH quakes I have experienced have been very mild, but some of the more recent quakes have been devastating. They do tend to get your attention, that is for certain. In this instance when Jesus died, I think God was inclined to mark the event with an emphasis to be remembered for an eternity. Of course, the significance of Jesus' death had different meanings to the various groups that were involved, the Phrases, the Sadducees, the disciples, the Sanhedrin, the Romans, and even king Herod! The perspective can be challenging unless, of course, you look beyond the grave to what Jesus was really teaching us. So, what does it take to get your attention?

GOD REACTS

CHAPTER 11
Shake THIS Earth!

Even in the Garden
God didn't pardon!

FROM MATTHEW 27:51 "AND BEHOLD, the veil of the temple was rent in two from the top to the bottom; and the earth did quake; and the rocks were rent." It is hard to imagine what God was trying to do with his earth creation at this moment. Maybe He is simply trying to draw our attention to this event about to take place. Maybe he is striking an exclamation mark on his strongest desire for His mankind creation. Shaking the earth just enough to remind us He has the power to do even more. The earth we count on for our sustenance through food for ourselves as well as food for the animals that serve as food for ourselves is capable of being shaken to its core if He wants. Shake the earth that was used to make man. The very foundation of all living things creation depends on to bring life was being shaken maybe, just maybe to get our attention.

Earth quakes are of no consequence in regions where no one exists. Just think about it! Qakes on the moon have no consequential effects to us here on earth. On the other hand, they wouldn't be called "earth" quakes would they? Moon quakes, Mars quakes, Saturn quakes, Venus quakes, etc. wouldn't send any kind of message to His mankind creation.

Now earth quakes, they get our attention. They can have devastating consequences. Tsunamis are also consequences of earth quakes and can leave devastating results. I was in a Roman town in Israel, Bet She'an, that had been partially excavated after being buried for centuries as the result of an earth quake. Entire columns from the fronts of buildings laying across the roadways, caved in roofs, toppled structures of all sorts were all present. The town was never rebuilt.

The picture at the end of this chapter shows the destruction that occurred to Bet She'an. The excavation that has taken place to show this destruction was amazing. The earth quake had occurred in 363 and has much archeological information written about it. This picture is mine from a trip we took in 2003. "Earthquakes in History and Archaeology/Israel Tours israel-tourguide.info", however, has pictures similar to the many pictures I took on that trip for further refence.

In this instance when Jesus was crucified, maybe the earth quake was marking the event; emphasizing the beginning of a new agreement between God and mankind. Even the solders reacted in the positive manner God was expecting:

> "Now the centurion, and they that were with him
> watching Jesus, when they saw the earthquake, and
> the things that were done, feared exceedingly, saying,
> 'Truly this was the Son of God.'"[1]

The Bible doesn't tell us anything about the devastation that undoubtedly took place as the result of the earth quake, but it does tell us about the damage to rocks. We will consider those rocks in the next chapter. But considering the damage earth quakes can do, I can imagine those in the immediate vicinity were more than just a little frightened. Adding fright on top of the anguish Jesus' followers were experiencing with the death of their messiah was not providing any reassurance to those who took part in Jesus' death. Maybe they had accomplished what they set out to accomplish and maybe not! Undoubtedly, those wanting Jesus dead were thinking they had managed to fulfill their objective until the curtain was torn and the earth quaked, and the rocks split. I can imagine they had second thoughts about their actions.

Jesus' crucifixion has several perspectives to consider. One perspective involves those who worked so hard to accomplish the dastardly deed. To them, they were removing a threat to what they perceived to be a satisfying and sound way of life the God they worshipped approved. They didn't want anything or anyone to shake up that relationship. They believed their righteousness so profoundly they would bring a life to an end to preserve it. Once they started the process, they were the only ones that could end it in their minds. For me it is very hard to imagine taking the life of anyone for any reason. Yet, the Pharisees and the Sadducees felt no way out except to kill this up start of a leader who was beginning to cause other people to think differently than they thought. It is difficult to imagine this opposition was so severe to their way of thinking the only way to resolve the conflict was to crucify Jesus. On the other hand, maybe life was so cheap that losing a life for their cause was worth the sinful nature it represented. Even then, they couldn't do it themselves legally; they had to enlist the services of the Romans, who they wanted removed from their society. Maybe their ulterior motive was to put the spotlight on their rulers to show the people the Roman rulers had to go. After all, it wasn't but a few years later the Romans had to put down a revolution and the Temple was destroyed completely in AD70 as a consequence[2]. Shaking the earth is part of how God manages to hold His creation together. Maybe these people needed to be reminded!

Jesus' followers had a second perspective. They were being led to think differently and in a convincing manner with all the miracles being committed to show them Jesus was speaking with authority. This new way of thinking about their relationship with the God they worshipped apparently was convincing considering the thousands in the country appearing to listen to Jesus. I can imagine their thoughts were ones of disappointment since Jesus apparently couldn't save himself from death. It's not hard for me to imagine the expectations these followers had as Jesus was sentenced to death and the death sentenced became a reality. It's not hard for me to visualize these followers trying to impose their will on the circumstances and realize how impotent they really were. There were others who came before Jesus who claimed to be the Messiah. They're deaths were always considered proof that they were false messiahs. It's not hard for me to imagine the uselessness they felt at being able to counteract the actions of a few considering how apparently easy it was for those few to see to it Jesus was hung on the cross. It's not hard for me to imagine the shaking of the earth they were experiencing being directed at them for not coming to the aid of Jesus. After all, Jesus was the only one making sense in the form of hope during those days of exploitation and Roman rule. It's not hard for me to imagine they wondered what more could they do to prevent this deed from taking place. It's not hard for me to imagine how helpless they felt in this situation. Especially when considering the fact that Jesus didn't want their help as evidenced by the reaction to Peter when he cut off the servant's ear when they arrested Jesus and Jesus healed it.[3] It's also not hard for me to imagine they didn't give themselves enough credit for what they could have done if they had sought God's input as Jesus had been teaching them.

The disciples, Jesus' closest companions, had a third perspective. They had been told over and over how this was going to happen. For example, just the week before Jesus was crucified while they were on their way to Jerusalem, Jesus was leading the way but talking with the disciples when he said:

> [31] And he took unto him the twelve, and said unto them, Behold, we go up to Jerusalem, and all the things that are written through the prophets shall be accomplished unto the Son of man. [32] For he shall be delivered up unto the Gentiles, and shall be mocked, and shamefully treated, and spit upon: [33] and they shall scourge and kill him: and the third day he shall rise again. [34] And they understood none of these things; and this saying was hid from them, and they perceived not the things that were said.[4]

yet they basically disappeared during the crucifixion until Sunday. He even predicted they would disappear:

> [32] "Behold, the hour cometh, yea, is come, that ye shall be scattered, every man to his own, and shall leave me alone: and *yet* I am not alone, because the Father is with me".[5]

This makes me wonder if they even felt the earth shake. However, I am certain they did, but they were probably so taken with grief they barely even recognized what had happened with the earth. They knew their great friend had been crucified and there was nothing they could do about it. I can imagine they must have felt very helpless. I know I do! SHAKE THIS EARTH! Wake me up. Lord!

QUESTIONS:

It has taken your life time to establish the basis that you use to judge what is happening in your world. Perhaps the word "discern" should be used instead of "judge" because passing judgement on something assumes that your ability to judge is infallible, whereas discerning the cause for your situation actually means you are ascertaining what is right (or wrong) about the matter. That foundation of discernment can be altered as reality is experienced and compared to expectations.

1. So, what does it take to get your attention?
2. Why do you think an earthquake occurred when Jesus died?
3. Do you think it was an intentional act that God caused?
4. How would you define the foundation of what you believe about God and about Jesus?
5. What would it take to change the foundation of your beliefs?
6. Have you ever experienced an earthquake first hand? How about second hand or has it been just through the news media? In any event, how would you relate the earthquake devastation

to what was being experienced in Jerusalem in the time of Jesus?

7. What kind of devastation was occurring? The earth's foundation or the foundation of what they believed?

8. Who was causing the devastation? The Pharisees? The Sadducees? The Sanhedrin? The Romans? The Disciples? Jesus? The people in general?

9. What is it today that is causing the foundation of what you believe to be shaken?

REFERENCES:

1. Mathew 27: 54
2. Flavius Josephus, *The Jewish War,* p. 303
3. Luke 22: 50 — 51
4. Luke 18:31 – 34
5. John 16:32

PRELUDE

WHAT IS IT ABOUT "ROCKS" that Mathew saw fit to mention them being split when Jesus died? Rocks were a major building commodity! Not only did they serve as structure, but, also, they were used for decorations and even for recording significant commandments! Perhaps God's consternation with those involved with Jesus' death was causing Him to send them a message they had not taken time to understand up until this moment!

CHAPTER 12

Split THIS Rock!

When I think of the rock of ages,
My mind goes to the Bible pages!

AGAIN, FROM MATTHEW 27:51 "AND behold, the veil of the temple was rent in two from the top to the bottom; and the earth did quake; and the rocks were rent." The Bible is full of God's attempt to clear the way for His mankind creation to worship only Him. The first five thousand years or so recorded in the Old Testament are constantly showing us how humankind finds God and then backslides to his own resources starting with Adam and Eve[1] all the way through the various good and bad kings[2], exile in Babylon, restoration back in Jerusalem[3], and then the subsequent foreign dominance from Alexander the Great, to finally the Romans. Humankind constantly seems to split their worship allegiance between God and self. When the one true God doesn't meet humankind's expectations, a god that will meet those expectations is "created"! The only constant in all of this is humankind's desire to worship something. One interesting fact in this consternation about creation is despite all our efforts to exist on our own, we somehow believe something extra-terrestrial exists controlling creation and deserves worship allegiance of some sort. This worship nature is seen with the Egyptian gods, Greek mythology, and with the Latin gods from the Romans. References to these "gods" can easily be found in the literature if anyone is interested. Even the Hebrews starting with

Abraham (Abram)[4] worshiped a god. It is a very good thing Abraham's god was God!

I can imagine God splitting the rock just to demonstrate humankind can be split just as easily as they split their worship allegiance. When one considers the essential matter of creation, the God we know made all kinds of creatures, and He made them for His own pleasure, but only one of those creatures, humankind, is capable of thanking Him for the creation they know. This thankfulness has to be the absolute essential beginning of worship. Is it any wonder when God considers His humankind creature, He expects to be acknowledged for what He has provided? Now He is confronted with an act from this humankind creature that must be counted as one of the greatest insults to His creativity that can possibly be rendered: crucifixion of His son! Splitting a rock must have a great significance. I can imagine God has at this point given up on His chosen people and that no matter what they say concerning His significance in their lives such as:

> Jehovah is my rock, and my fortress, and my deliverer;

> My shield, and the horn of my salvation, my high tower.[5]

And

> But Jehovah hath been my tower,
> And my God the rock of my refuge.[6]

Splitting the rock makes me wonder if He believes it anymore!

Israel is a very rocky place. In fact, on our visit there not too long ago, our guide described the region as God's dumping ground for all the rocks of the world. Splitting those rocks would definitely be matters of concern to those who were witnessing Christ's crucifixion.

Jesus considered himself as the foundation of our faith and urged us to believe our faith in him is as solid as the rock referenced in those Psalms[7]. When God splits those rocks as a response to the crucifixion of His son, I can imagine He is telling us we are the ones who have destroyed the foundation of all creation. We, His humankind creatures, are the destroyers of the faith needed for us to exist without anxiety, without fear, without concern for others, without love, and without relationships. With this foundation destroyed, God is challenging us to find our way in His creation as the Humans we were originally created to be. I think God knows fulfilling this challenge is impossible. I also think God knows one other secret; a secret so profound it is impossible to believe without faith. Torn curtains, earthquakes, and split rocks are nothing in comparison to the secret He is about to reveal. God can control his universe, but He needs His humankind creatures, the only creatures that can thank Him for His creation, to accept He alone deserves the humankind worship as reflected in the acknowledgement He is seeking.

Now He is splitting the symbol of his steadfast love, the ROCK!. God the father and Christ, the son; two of the three making up the holy trinity. Splitting the rock could very well mean He is showing a new phase of our relationship with Him is about to take place. Splitting the rock could mean God is splitting our faith foundation so "the son" has as much significance in our faith as He does. Splitting the foundation of our faith can definitely be a significant aspect of the events taking place as God responds to the crucifixion of His son.

One might think God has given up on the Jewish people to accomplish the task of bringing the reality of His existence to "all the nations[8]", especially when you read the Old Testament from cover to cover.

> "[18]and in thy seed shall all the nations of the earth be blessed; because thou hast obeyed my voice."

God has tried and tried to convince His chosen people it is worth their while to depend on Him for all things, to acknowledge Him as The Creator, and to give Him all the Glory for any accomplishments achieved.

Just the opposite might be considered. Indeed, God is fulfilling his plan, not giving up on it! His plan all along has been to have His humankind creation choose right over wrong, good over evil, life over death; and to make that choice on their own. He always wants His mankind creation with Him. The problem is He cannot have imperfection. Not only that, He cannot even accept any imperfect performances of any kind because He cannot give credence to imperfection of any sort. He must have undistracted devotion. Anything less does nothing but give credibility to less than perfection which is unacceptable in His domain. Obviously, achieving this with free will has not been the way to go. Achieving this with a chosen people to demonstrate how to accomplish the task has not worked either. Now it is time to pull out all the stops to both fix the problem and provide a way to make it possible for His humankind creatures to atone for their transgressions and be acceptable in His sight. Only perfection and nothing less can accomplish this task. The only way to prove His way is best is to defeat death. To accomplish this feat, He must split the foundation and share the task with that portion of Himself that is human. The completion of this task accomplishes three goals: it demonstrates the extent of His love for His humankind creatures; it provides a means for His Humankind creatures to atone for their lack of perfection with the acceptance of His son as the one who bears their sin; and it shows the tree of life[9] that existed in the Garden of Eden has always been available, is always available, and that death has no hold over eternity. Split THIS rock if you can!

QUESTIONS:

Biblical references to "The Rock" usually imply the basis for our faith. To appreciate what our basis of our faith really is, I think we need to take stock of what it is that we live our life to achieve. I also think most of us would agree we do not have a single point of reference to serve as the basis of what we consider to be important. I submit we have various sources of reference we use depending on the circumstances.

How we split our lives between God and worldly endeavors is the matter at hand we need to address in this chapter.

1. What in your mind constitutes worship?
2. Can you think of something in your life to cause you to exaggerate its importance to a level of worship?
3. Do you think you could be accused of splitting your worship between God and something else?
4. What does it mean in your mind to have Jesus as your rock?
5. How do you split your worship between God, the Son, and the Holy Spirit?
6. Do you think there was a time that God gave up on you because of your worship practices?
7. What atonement do you think is needed to prevent you from splitting your centers of worship?
8. How perfect do you think you have to be to gain the benefits given to you through Jesus' sacrifice?
9. What aspect of Jesus' crucifixion do you think can't be split?

REFERENCES:

1. Genesis 2:7 through 3:24
2. 1Kings; 2Kings;1Chronicles; and 2Chronicles
3. Ezra, Nehemiah, and Malachi
4. Genesis 12
5. Psalm 18: 2
6. Psalm 94: 22
7. Matthew 7: 24 – 27
8. Genesis 22: 18
9. Genesis 2: 9

PRELUDE

JESUS SPENT 3 DAYS SOMEWHERE after he died and before he was seen in his resurrected life. What he did in those three days made it right with God for those who had passed into death before his time. But it also cleared the path for the rest of us to be right with God. Jesus said, "Destroy this temple, and in three days I will raise it up" (John 2:19). The people of his time thought he was talking about Herod's Temple, but he was talking about something even more amazing; That is the restoration of life! From my perspective, I am amazed it only took 3 days to make things right for me with God!

So, He sent His only begotten Son to show us how much He loves His creation. He also provided a means to expiate, make amends, for the deviation we manage from the perfection He expects. The problem is our experience (in the form of our imagination) does not include the reality of the perfection He requires nor does our imagination permit us to comprehend how our deviation from perfection can be made right with the Creator. The only way this right relationship can be created is to accept by faith the resolution given to us in the form of Jesus Christ, his death, and his resurrection.

Yet, Jesus was only gone three days. So, what was Christ doing for three days? If he was dead but wasn't dead, where did he go? What did he do? And how did he get back? Quite frankly, I have no experience to even begin to be able to imagine any kind of answer to these questions. However, the Bible does tell us he spent at least part of that time in "the place of the dead" and he rescued the spirits of the saints that had died before him[5, 6]. Even so, it is still amazing it only took three days for Christ to make things right for us with God. You would think with all the worldly experiences we have, it would take considerably longer. God's grace is forever and apparently very lenient as well. The hardest part is accepting "that" grace sufficiently to recognize we have the courage, the knowledge, the wisdom, and the will to live according to His will.

We really need to realize God's grace is forever! Jesus' brother tries to help with this understanding when he states[7]:

> [4] Ye adulteresses, know ye not that the friendship of the world is enmity with God? Whosoever therefore would be a friend of the world maketh himself an enemy of God. [5] Or think ye that the scripture speaketh in vain? Doth the spirit which he made to dwell in us long unto envying? [6] But he giveth more grace. Wherefore *the scripture* saith, God resisteth the proud, but giveth grace to the humble."

I think all of us can accept that earth was created. This creation isn't hard to imagine because earth is where we exist, and creation is all around us. Accepting God accomplished this creation and created a "heaven" as well does require an imagination that goes way beyond normal when we consider the reality of our existence. For some reason, living in this creation means we feel obligated to change the created conditions to suit our purposes. I submit, if instead of creating conditions in our world to suit our purposes, we accept the created conditions for our purposes, it would be easier to accept the world as it was created for us and, therefore, accept that the world has a Creator.

Jesus sacrificed himself so we would accept the grace of God to forgive us for trying to create our world in His world (or is it we are trying to create His world in our world. That is the dichotomy isn't it?). The three days it took for Christ to make things right for us with God is definitely a wonder for our imagination. The kind of experience he had to go through during those three days to make up for the sins I (we) have committed, in my imagination at least, must have been considerably concentrated. Definitely, the agony was way beyond what I could possibly endure. How much gratitude I owe Jesus is also way beyond what I can imagine. The least I can do is try very very hard to live the rest of my life as close to perfect as I can in a manner that represents Jesus' example as I understand it. Such a task is, also, way beyond my imagination, especially since I live in the world He loves so much He gave His only begotten son to save it[8]! Since I am who I am, living like Jesus is not in my nature, but I can live such a way that others can see Jesus through me. The question becomes: is the person others see when they see me, me or Jesus?

The concept of "hades" complicates this issue just a bit. Did Jesus suffer in hades? Is hades as we have supposed? Was this "hades" or 'Sheol' (a Hebrew word that means the abode of the dead)?

Hades in the apostle's Creed is a concept that evolved during the 'intertestamental' period. You won't find it in the Old Testament because it is actually pagan in origin. It says he entered there to 'set the captives free' or that he 'led a train of captives toward liberty'. I am not sure exactly what it means for Jesus to descend to hades or what hades is exactly. I imagine Jewish folks thought of it more as 'sheol' which is a type of holding place for the dead in their beliefs.

At the beginning of this chapter, I mentioned the Apostle's Creed and how it came into existence. With the background just presented, it seems appropriate to repeat the Creed so we can understand more fully at this moment what it is we have accepted on faith in order to be right with the Creator God:

THE APOSTLES' CREED9

(Ecumenical Version)

> I believe in God the Father Almighty, Maker of heaven and earth:

> I believe in Jesus Christ his only Son, our Lord; who was conceived by the Holy Ghost, born of the virgin Mary, suffered under Pontius Pilate, was crucified, dead, and buried; he descended into hell; the third day he rose again from the dead; he ascended into heaven, where he is seated at the right hand of God the Father Almighty; from thence he shall come to judge the quick and the dead.

> I believe in the Holy Ghost; the holy catholic church; the communion of saints; the forgiveness of sins; the resurrection of the body; and the life everlasting. Amen

We remember Jesus died for our sins, but it is much more than that. He paid for our sins and went to hades for us. He also went to hades to save those that had died before his crucifixion, so they would be included in eternal life. Three days in hades just don't seem to be enough in comparison to what we really deserve!

QUESTIONS:

I am certain no argument would occur if I were to say that none of us actually knows what happens when we die. What happens to our being, our essence, that part of who we are which we can't really define? What we "believe" happens and what will really happen will not be revealed until it happens! That hasn't stopped us from putting forth our thoughts about what will happen and why.

1. Jesus died on Friday and came back to life three days later. What do you think was happening in those three days?
2. What do you think happens to the accumulated knowledge, experience, and wisdom a person acquires during his or her lifetime after that person dies?
3. Where does "faith" come into effect with the aspect of death?
4. Can you imagine the amount of faith Jesus required to believe he would come back from death after three days as he predicted?
5. What aspect of your life do you think has deviated from the perfection that you think God expects from you?
6. The word expiation means to make amends. What aspect of your life do you think requires you to make amends with God?
7. What aspects of your life do you think you have no worries about making amends with God?
8. How do you think Jesus' death and resurrection makes up for what you can't accomplish with your effort to make amends?
9. The Apostle's Creed states what we believe about the individual entities of the Holy Trinity, is there any aspect about this Creed that requires more faith to believe than any other aspect?

REFERENCES:

1. http://www.newadvent.org/cathen/01629a.htm
2. 1 Peter 3:19

3. Mathew 12:40
4. Genesis 3:5
5. Mathew 27:52
6. 1 Peter 3:19
7. James 4:4-6
8. John 3:16
9. http://www.crivoice.org/creedsearly.html

PRELUDE

So, Jesus died and was placed in a tomb. Now what? I can't imagine the anguish the disciples were experiencing! But here is the deal; each of us has thought about their experiences and have come to our own conclusions. In fact, we have so personalized the experience of Jesus' death with respect to what we know and understand that we have divided ourselves into umpteen gillion different sects in order to find others who agree with what we have finally resolved in our own minds about Jesus' death and resurrection. Amazing isn't it? The "Church" that was born because of the life and death of Jesus is so partitioned we all have something we can relate to even if we can't agree on what aspect we should concentrate. We agree, however, Jesus lived, and Jesus died, and Jesus lives again!

CHAPTER 14
Lay In THIS Tomb

Whoever made up the word "tomb"
Must have been thinking the opposite would be "womb"!

THE BIBLE TELLS US JOSEPH from Arimathea was a rich man[1] who
went to Pilot to get permission to take Jesus' body. He then "loaned"
his new tomb for Jesus' burial. He wrapped the body of Jesus in a clean
cloth and laid it in his tomb. I can remember reading this when I was
a youngster and reading about how Joseph rolled a great stone to the
door of the tomb[2].

A few years ago I visited the holy land and saw some examples
of the way in which the tombs were constructed in Jesus' day. As the
bible says, these tombs were hewn in the rock and consisted of a very
small cave like structure just barely big enough for a small raised rock
platform for resting the body with very little overhead space. The rock
that was rolled in front of the door was a round slab or disc like rock
that was about a foot thick and probably six feet in diameter. This
disc actually stood on the round edge and was rolled in a trough to
seal the doorway. The bible tells us that Jesus' body was in the tomb
before sundown on Friday when the Sabbath began (although it doesn't
specifically state "Friday") through the Sabbath and until dawn of the
first day of the week[3].

Considering the "final" nature of a "tomb", it isn't difficult to
imagine the disciples abandoned Jesus. In fact, only John was at the

cross[4] and no disciples were at the tomb, only Mary Magdalene and "the other Mary" the wife of Clopas[5, 6]. We really don't know what went on in that tomb except as best as we can determine, Jesus wasn't there (see Chapter 13). None the less, the confining nature of a tomb has many considerations for us to contemplate.

Ordinarily, Jesus' body would be going through the normal rages of death converting back to nature. Something much more important than this conversion was occurring and it wasn't the conversion of Jesus' body back to nature. Instead, his disciples were morning his demise and were going through their own conversion. Basically, they were converting back to what they were before Jesus called them. It isn't difficult to imagine they were struggling with conflict. Can you imagine the questions? What have we spent the last three years doing? What are we supposed to do now? Why didn't we manage to save him from this awful death? What more could we have done? Who do we need to see to protect ourselves from a similar fate? Are we in danger? Where should we go, what should we do? Can we go back to the work we were doing before we joined up with Jesus? I am certain these questions are not even close to what insecurity and anxiety feeling the disciples were experiencing.

At the same time I can imagine, in their minds, the disciples could visualize Jesus' life had come to an end and all they had been experiencing for the last three years was now finished. All the lessons they had learned were not the foremost thoughts in their minds, let alone thoughts about how to implement those lessons. They had been given powers[7] they didn't know they could use without Jesus. Now, without Jesus, how were they supposed to use them?

Jesus' death didn't happen without warning[8]. In fact, the last time he had told them of his impending death was just a week earlier[9]. Still, the final nature of death was what they knew. Undoubtedly, they could not see beyond their loss. I can imagine they could not visualize life beyond the tomb. I really don't see how we can blame them! None of us has any experience beyond the tomb! After all, how final can it get?

We know from two thousand years of history, however, this tomb wasn't final. This tomb was the start of something, not the end of something. Whatever happened in that tomb was more than miraculous! There is no way we can imagine in any way shape or form how Jesus managed to overcome the death he had experienced, a death that turned into life. Jesus had brought back to life a young girl[10] earlier in his crusade and of course, he had brought Lazarus back to life[11] just a short time earlier. These actions are hard enough to believe, but bringing himself back to life, wow, how did he manage that? There shouldn't be any doubt that Jesus died! He was hung on a cross until he stopped breathing and then stabbed in the chest just to make certain[12]. There are outside sources that attest to Jesus death as well, like Josephus[13].

The "tombs" we are laid in when we die are much different than a cave hewn in a rock. Some are in six-foot-deep holes, some are on top of the ground, and some are nothing more than an urn to hold our ashes. No matter where they are, we know beyond a doubt they are the final resting place for our earthly bodies. There is no coming back from these tombs. Is it any wonder we have some degree of skepticism about what went on in Jesus' tomb? None the less, whatever it was, its significance has endured for over two thousand years.

I have often thought the whole episode of Jesus' death and resurrection was a hoax, but not in the manner we would ordinarily think of a hoax. Jesus willingly (well almost willingly) went through with all these acts of his sacrifice because he and his Father new a secret. They knew the tomb would not hold Jesus. God had this in His plan all along. That is the hoax. He knew we would be contemplating this act for a long, long time. The significance of this act has not waned one bit, not even a little bit. In fact, the significance has grown beyond what those original 12 could possibly have contemplated especially at the moment Jesus was placed in that tomb.

Although we have taken the events that happened in those three days and twisted them every which way we can, one fact remains, Jesus overcame death. The twisting still continues, but so does the significance. We may attach different meanings to those events, but it is just us humans trying to put these events into a perspective that our individual nature can understand. We pick on those facets of Jesus life and death we can relate to our understanding of matters. In actuality, we have no way to understand with our limited experiences with life what took place in that tomb or during those three days. In a manner of speaking, each of us has our own interpretation of what transpired in that tomb. So, we find others with whom we can commune that have a similar understanding. When we make a community out of those that have similar understanding, we call it a congregation and a church is born. The twisting has made many different churches or denominations, but one fact remains. Jesus tomb was not permanent. The rock was rolled away and a new way of living with God was introduced.

There is no one to blame for Jesus' death. It was planned because of the secret that God knew. He knew His son's death was inevitable. He knew the tomb would not hold Jesus. That was His hoax. He also knew Jesus' defeat of death would be the ultimate sacrifice and His love for mankind would be exemplified because of placing Jesus in that tomb. His love was so great He was willing to allow mankind to go through the agony of realizing what they had done to His son was the ultimate in sin! But more importantly, if one really thinks about it, it was the ultimate in forgiveness. Without the tomb and the inability for the tomb to hold Jesus, there would be no forgiveness, there would be no means to experience grace, there would be no way to experience hope, there would be no way to experience unconditional love!

In deed, this was Jesus' tomb, not ours. Lay in THIS tomb, if you can!

QUESTIONS:

I don't know about you, but for me dead is supposed to be dead! But Jesus taught us that death is not as final as we might think. He knew that the tomb would not be his last stop, yet, his disciples thought it was! Amazing isn't it? But here is something to rationalize: we still have a lot of graveyards around and they are not empty. Where did the essence of those people go?

George M. Goodrich

1. What was going through the disciple's minds when Jesus actually died?
2. What was this confinement intended to accomplish?
3. Were the Sabbath requirements honored?
4. What was happening to Jesus' body during these "three days"?
5. Why do you think the matter of Jesus' death and resurrection has endured for over 2000 years?
6. First, we kill Jesus, then we put him in a tomb; next he comes back to life. Which of these three events is the most difficult to rationalize? Why?
7. The tomb should have been the last we heard from Jesus, did the disciples think so as well? How do we know this?
8. If Jesus really overcame death, why did the stone need to be rolled away?
9. What aspect of this tomb event constitutes "God's Grace"?

REFERENCES:

1. Mathew 27:57
2. Mathew 27:60
3. Mathew 28:1
4. John 19:26
5. Mathew 27:61
6. John 19:25
7. Mathew 10:1
8. Mathew 16:21, 17:22
9. Mark 20: 17 - 19
10. Mathew 9:18-26
11. John 11:38-44
12. John 19:32-34
13. Josephus "Testimonium Flavianum" (-*Jewish Antiquities*, **18.3.3 §63** (Based on the translation of Louis H. Feldman, The Loeb Classical Library.))

110

PRELUDE

I THINK THE REACTION TO Jesus' death and resurrection must have caused his disciples to have astounding disbelief. What were they thinking? It doesn't seem to me they would have been thinking this was a sacrifice! It must have taken considerable time for them to realize what their function should be after these remarkable events occurred. Somehow, they managed to realize the significance of everything Jesus had been teaching them. The concept of God making a sacrifice of His son was totally way beyond where their minds might have taken them. "In Remembrance of me" became the standard to live by and the realization that His blood had been sacrificed for all of mankind became the center of the message they began to preach to the world.

CHAPTER 15

Put THIS Blood on Your Door Posts!

Why do we sacrifice?
It really doesn't seem very nice.

VERY EARLY IN THE BIBLE, blood in God's creation was recognized as being essential to life![1] Hummmm, certainly makes sense to me! In fact, God forbid consuming it and if it was shed, He required an "accounting"[2]. By "accounting", I think God meant that matters had to be corrected or made right. It is easy to imagine that blood had great importance and great significance. Blood was recognized as being essential to nature; its life-giving properties were well understood. So much so that the loss of blood required the need to make matters right with God should it be shed. An accounting was required. It is not difficult to imagine how this accounting became part of rituals when blood was shed. It is also not difficult to imagine that making matters right with God required giving something up in return. Yet, mankind's needs for sustenance and protection from the elements required living things to give up their life. In fact, God allowed human kind to sacrifice animals for sustenance purposes while He was making His point about the significance of blood[3]. Considering this understanding of the word sacrifice, it is not hard to imagine how bloodletting became a ritualistic part of making matters right with God. Sacrifice requires something be given up to realize a benefit. When blood is involved, in other words when life is given, the sacrifice becomes a blood sacrifice. This sacrificial practice has several aspects that cause us to wonder about its effectiveness and the ability of the act to correct the wrongs between God and man. Did the sacrifices really accomplish what they were intended to accomplish? If yes, why did they have to do it repeatedly? Somewhere along the line these sacrifices became a significant part of worship or were the sacrifices another way to justify what mankind really wanted to do with their worldly possessions. Perhaps, the act of sacrificing became associated with matters that were in accordance with the good things in life and were repeated to experience the good feelings over again.

God performed the first blood sacrifice when He made coats of skin[4] for Adam and Eve. God sacrificed animals, so Adam and Eve could be protected from the elements. For the animals to be sacrificed, they had to be dispatched thus causing the first blood to be let making this first sacrifice a blood sacrifice. This act was after Adam and Eve had received their punishment for disobeying Him. This first sacrifice was atonement for the sin Adam and Eve committed, except, it was God performing the act rather than man. It may not seem to be a sacrifice as we normally experience this act; just the same, animals had to be killed for God to provide the skins for the coats. It is significant that up until then, Adam and Eve didn't require clothing. Their disobedience put them in harm's way, so animals were sacrificed for their protection from the harm, namely the elements. Of course, God may simply have offered the clothing to cover their sin as well.

"Sacrifice" throughout the Bible is a means for atoning for sins that are committed against God or for atonement because mankind did not comply with God's directions. These directions were for honoring God and for living amongst each other. Honoring God forbid them from substituting for God or for defaming Him. The directions for living amongst each other were mainly common-sense commands that put relationships first.

The most notorious sacrifice recorded in the Old Testament part of the Bible, at least in my opinion, was the sacrifice the Egyptians were required to make for wanting to keep the Hebrew people as slaves. The Egyptians were required to put up with many disasters, but this "most notorious" sacrifice was God's act of sacrificing their first born[5]. The first time I read the account of this historical event, I was appalled at the gruesome nature of the act. Yet, I was also astounded with the power it took to accomplish the act. It was very hard for me to imagine that the God I know would go to such extremes to convince the Egyptians they needed to free the Hebrews. However, the reaction of the Egyptians to this request for the Hebrew freedom apparently required this action for God to be convincing. I was even more astounded because God told the Hebrews to take advantage of their "good" relationship with their Egyptian neighbors. These "good neighbors" "gave them favor"[6] to the point the Egyptian gave the Hebrews their gold and silver[7] and probably much of the livestock the Hebrews took with them. These two acts just don't seem to fit together, but then God works in ways far beyond ordinary understanding. Perhaps the Egyptians simply were glad to be rid of the Hebrews after all the catastrophes that the Hebrew "god" had created!

In this story when the Egyptians actually "sacrificed their first born", God told the Hebrews to make yet another blood sacrifice: each family unit was to kill a lamb and put the blood from the lamb on their two doorposts and lintels. They were also supposed to consume the lambs in their entirety before dawn. In this way, God would "pass over"[8] the Hebrews and their first born would be spared.

God directed the Hebrews to keep reenacting these sacrificial events from the first Passover as a memorial and to make the event an annual celebration to God[9].

When we read the accounts of Jesus demise in the Gospels, we learn Jesus and the disciples were celebrating this Passover event just prior to Jesus being arrested. In fact, the bread and wine we partake during our communion were part of the sadder meal that for centuries had been the center of the commemoration tradition for the Passover celebration. This Passover event was intended to remind the Hebrew people of what it took to free them from slavery to the Egyptians.

The symbolism of the Passover, of the lamb sacrifice, of the covenant between God and the Hebrew people, of the blood, and of the bread, the unleavened bread, has much more significance considering Jesus' death and resurrection. In this instance, instead of the first born being saved from death, the first born "lamb" of God gives his life[10], his blood, so the rest of us can be saved. Instead of the blood being put on the door post and lentil, it is declared as a new covenant[11] between God and mankind and then it is drunk. Instead of bread being eaten in such a hurry it doesn't have time to be leavened, it is a symbol of a broken body[12]. A body so broken it becomes a sacrifice all by itself. Once again, just like the first sacrifice, God is making the sacrifice. Only this time, God is sacrificing Himself. Instead of being freed from the Egyptians, the resurrection guarantees death is not permanent[13] or life is freed from death. What's more, this resurrection guarantees that God the Father accepted Jesus' sacrifice and qualifies all the teaching and promises Jesus made.

Now that the Passover has a new meaning. The last blood sacrifice has taken place, and a new covenant exists. I can imagine what it means to celebrate this event, to commemorate the inception, to appreciate a new challenge for the Passover. I can imagine the instigator of this new covenant has become the epitome of how we are to live our lives to be at one with God without making any more blood sacrifices.

I heard a story on the internet where a young boy by the name of Logan experienced a life changing revelation when he had to dispatch a sick calf[14]. The whole point is Logan had to put down his calf because it had a broken back due to no fault of the calf. The fault was the lack of nutrition because the calf's mother did not have "good" milk. It is hard to imagine how devastating it was for him to endure the fact a death had to occur because the calf had a broken back. Logan goes on to equate this experience to the difficulties he imagines God had when He had to "put His son down". (Note: The notion that Logan had difficulty "imaging" God's difficulty was the impetus for me to use my imagination throughout this book.) It isn't really too hard to imagine what God was thinking considering what we experience in todays life situations, but still, what was so broken He had to give up his only son.

How much are we broken? Are we broken enough that God must give up His only son to fix our problem? The "problem", "brokenness", is our relationship with God. So, how did it break and how did Christ's death fix it? Obviously, killing the calf didn't fix its broken back, but it did relieve the calf from its suffering! So, does God's sacrificing His son fix our brokenness or does it just relieve us from suffering?

Perhaps the fact we are still here even after we killed Jesus tells us just how much God trusts that the last blood sacrifice was made so we can understand that our brokenness does not have to separate us from God. Perhaps the facts that Jesus only spent three days in hades; that there was only three hours of darkness; that only the curtain was torn; that the earth was only shaken; and that the rocks were only split means hope for oneness with God still exists. For all the sins I have committed, Jesus could have spent another lifetime in hades. As far as darkness is concerned, it isn't hard to imagine we are surrounded by darkness because of the sins we committed and are still committing. It isn't hard to imagine a significant tear exists in our relationship with God and this tear is way beyond a torn curtain. It isn't hard to imagine a considerable shake up in our attitude would be required to make our existence compatible with God; a shake-up that can't be simulated by a meager earth quake. And split rocks: how can we possibly imagine the rock that represents our oneness with God could be so easily split!

God created us and it is that creation that makes it possible to be at one with Him. His son, Jesus, not only showed us how to live with each other, Jesus also showed us how to live with God. He showed us even death cannot separate us from God. So, YES, put HIS BLOOD on your door and live a life that reflects the oneness we have with God.

QUESTIONS:

We all know what it means to sacrifice, at least I think we all know what it means! Still, the question of how sacrificing something to make us "right with God" has a mysterious aspect about it that has confounded me and probably many others. Jesus' blood was shed as a sacrifice for all our sins and God says we don't have to wonder about it. We just need to accept it! WOW!

1. What constitutes a wrong against God?
2. Why do you think a sacrifice was necessary to atone for the wrongs done against God?
3. For that matter, what constitutes a sacrifice?
4. If God is the creator (and He is) what can we give Him that isn't already His to make amends for our wrongs?
5. What were the rituals God had asked the Hebrews to repeat to commemorate their release from slavery intended to accomplish?
6. How do you know you have been forgiven after you have participated in the sacrifice ritual?
7. Does God's sacrificing His son fix our brokenness or does it just relieve us from suffering?
8. What similarities exist between the Jewish "Passover" and the death and resurrection of Jesus Christ?
9. How does Jesus' death make things right between you and God?

REFERENCES:

1. Genesis 9:4
2. Genesis 9:5
3. Genesis 9:3
4. Genesis 3:21
5. Exodus 11:5
6. Exodus 11:3
7. Exodus 11:2
8. Exodus 12:13
9. Exodus 12:14
10. Mark 15:37
11. Mark 14:24
12. Mark 14:22
13. Mark 16:6
14. https://www.youtube.com/watch?v=zCdZwitrNoY

PRELUDE

FAITH, HOPE, AND LOVE, AND how they are entwined with sacrifice presents an interesting challenge. More specifically how they are entwined with God's sacrifice can be a conundrum. The challenge is to understand the relationship between faith, hope, love, and sacrifice. Then we need to add the notion that God made a sacrifice to achieve His goal to prove His love just to begin to understand the conundrum.

CHAPTER 16
Sacrifice THIS Life

Is giving up a life for mine
Really what God had in mind?

CHAPTER 16 CONSIDERS THE MEANING of sacrifice and what had to be done to accomplish the freedom of the Hebrews. Still, this sacrifice is confusing, at least for me! First, I have difficulty understanding how this sacrifice is supposed to accomplish the task of making my life right with God. Apparently, I am not alone in trying to understand this act, because much has been written that tries to explain the theoretical aspects of the how this atonement is accomplished[1]. I have nothing to offer in the way of explaining how God intended this sacrifice to work or explaining how Christ's death and resurrection will physically manage to make everything right between each of us and God. However, I can imagine one day we all will experience this great understanding. The Bible tells us we don't know it all yet, only part. However, in those same verses, Paul tells us faith, hope and love abide, and love is the greatest ("reason" I suspect)[2]. We can appreciate how much love is involved with this sacrificial act given that God must love us emphatically, since Jesus death was not met with the retribution prescribed in His law[3]. The hope and the faith parts require much more understanding to appreciate.

Hope suggests we need to live beyond the understanding in a state of wonder and expectations. One part of this word leaves us wondering rather than experiencing the wonder. We wonder if we are hoping that what we have been led to believe is entirely true. I can imagine the hope part being that we definitely hope our sins will be forgiven because if they are not forgiven, our understanding of the consequences is a miserable afterlife.

The faith part has many other implications. Besides having the faith that the sacrifice was indeed successful, we have learned to use faith in many other aspects of our life. Faith means we believe in something despite the fact we don't have positive proof of that something. Faith exists in many aspects of our life and we need not look far before we see its ramifications. Putting this daily faith into an example, just think of the faith we have when driving that the oncoming car will stay in its lane and not have a head on collision with us as we pass each other. That kind of faith is experienced in all aspects of our life. Faith that the electricity will be there when we switch on the light; faith that the ladder will hold us up as we climb (although my friend, Ollen, may have lost his faith in ladders since a rung broke while he was climbing on one); faith that the people who prepare our food in a restaurant do it with utmost sanitary care; faith that we will not be challenged beyond what we can bear. In the instance with Christ being sacrificed for us, the faith we need is that eternal life will transpire. The most amazing part of all three of these words, faith, hope, and love is that believing is all we need to do[4]. Wow!

In "Adventures with Apples and Snakes from the Garden of Eden"[5], I put forth a formula that indicates our existence depends on the outcome of a relationship between experience, expectations, and reality. The relationship starts with expectations and depends upon our experience and reality.

$$\text{Expectations} = \text{Experience} + \text{Reality}$$
$$\text{Or}$$
$$\text{Experience} = \text{Expectations} - \text{Reality}$$
$$\text{Or}$$
$$\text{Reality} = \text{Expectations} - \text{Experience}$$

Because of our experience with living as humans, the reality of our situation doesn't give us much confidence in faith or hope beyond our everyday existence. I can honestly say the same does not apply to "love". Even as obtuse as our emotions about love may be, I believe I am closer to the significance of love than I am to faith or hope.

I have experienced love from both directions; giving and receiving. First of all, I truly believe God loves me. I also believe my wife of 56 years loves me as do all three of my children. God's love is all around me and my family's love is ever before me. Giving love in return is easy. Giving love to my fellow Christians is easy as well. Loving my enemies, however, is a little harder, but just the same, I am convinced I can and I do. I am certain my nature makes it difficult for some to love me, just as the nature of some others makes it difficult for me to love them. I am also certain that perhaps even my children at times have had difficulties loving me. I <u>hope</u> they do love me and I have <u>faith</u> they will if they don't. Still, I have no control over their emotions. This "lack of control" is why my confidence in faith and hope is lacking. I am also certain about the love that exists between my wife and me. I am certain she loves me, just as I am certain she knows I love her. I will admit though, she probably has more difficulties loving me than I have loving her. I guess that is why there is always hope and faith!

But I digress! The issue of Christ being sacrificed for me, for my sins, for my life, has me beyond awe! In fact, the entire issue of sacrificing has me examining the whole matter. Where did this need for sacrifice originate? I submit mankind in the beginning must have felt that somehow matters went better for them when a sacrifice of some sort was made. I wonder if maybe somehow an experience occurred such that an event that tested a skill went better when a personal sacrifice was made before the event. Perhaps a coincidence occurred where a certain skill was thought to be enhanced after a pig was slaughtered. I am just guessing, of course, but yet, there must have been a huge transition between a coincidental occurrence and the occurrence of giving up a life to achieve the enhancement! From my perspective, the God I believe is the creator doesn't need to be given anything, because He already has it all. It must be our imagination that leads us to think we need to sacrifice something to Him to make matters right between us? This same imagination makes us think we can atone for our transgressions by making a sacrifice! To me, sacrifice is a cheap way out! To make "things right" between God and me must first assume matters are not right between me and God.

What is wrong between us is the same thing that gets wrong between me and my fellow man. I don't honor him; I think I am better than he is; I look out for myself before I look out for him; I want what he has; I take his things just because I need them more than I think he needs them; I use his talents to better my position with respect to others; I degrade him in front of others to make myself look better; I adamantly insist I know a better way; I consider my knowledge to represent the wisest in all matters; I believe my experience gives me an advantage; I consider my status to be better than his; I must be first in line to show others how to do it; my way is always better than his; and on and on and on! The sacrifice that needs to be made to make these matters right with God is the sacrifice of thought; the sacrifice of intention; the sacrifice of attention; the sacrifice of will; the sacrifice of want; the sacrifice of need; the sacrifice of self-preservation; the sacrifice of just about everything we consider necessary for our perception of existence. Sacrificing some property thing we own is a long way from achieving what is really needed to make matters right between me and God. In this light I have a challenging time imagining how sacrificing Jesus' life makes up for all of this. I suspect this means I am missing a very important and significant factor! After all, I have already told you I have accepted Jesus Christ as my personal savior, so something essential is obviously missing!

Rationalizing this further, I have come to understand if I am to accept Jesus Christ's ability to "save me" I must try to implement the attribute of Jesus' relationship with God to my own life. So, let's look at what Jesus was trying to teach his disciples (and us). The attributes Jesus portrayed in his brief time here on earth are so far reaching that over 2000 years have been spent by many much more eloquent than I am explaining them. However, in the most meaningful way I can think of here are my thoughts. He came to serve and not to be served[6]. He taught we need to develop the right spirit or driving force; he taught we need to be mindful of others especially those who consider others more important than themselves; he taught we need to be respectful of our surroundings and especially of the role God played in their creation; he taught we need to strive to live righteously; he taught we need to have compassion for others; he taught we need to be pure in our thinking; he taught we need to be advocating peace; he taught persecution for trying to be righteous is to be expected; he taught we all are important to God[7]! He also taught implementing these attributes into our lives goes beyond what the law taught[8].

The adage of conducting our lives in such a manner that others will see Jesus through us is the sacrifice that must be made. Our sacrifice should be to give up our desire to promote ourselves and to transform our lives into ones that reflect our understanding of what God expects of us in the way we behave and act towards others. This sacrifice is real to me! The only way to achieve it is to try. The only way to try is to steep oneself in the word God gave us in the book called the Bible. The best way for steeping ourselves in the word is to remember the New Testament was not written when Jesus walked the earth and to remember it was his example of how he encountered other people we should "try" to emulate. The sacrifice he made had to serve as the example we needed to follow as the New Testament! He was the living example of how to live a life God considered essential to be right with Him. For us to believe the intention and to believe Jesus was this example, Jesus had to be sacrificed so his resurrection could prove he was, indeed, The Example!

The issue is whether the war that goes on between our physical needs and wants and our spiritual needs and wants can find the correct alignment. It isn't difficult to imagine that giving in to the physical aspects of our existence takes away from the spiritual aspects of our existence. The difficulty I have is that the physical aspects have a way of demanding attention the spiritual aspects don't. I mean, hunger, shelter, clothing, bodily needs, sexual drive, and even the desire to achieve are important aspects of our existence. The desire to love one another, serve one another, honor relationships, experience the Creator in a hallowed way, worship the Creator for what He has done are examples of spiritual needs that at times seem to be secondary to the physical needs our bodies seem to demand. Putting this battle into the perspective that the spiritual aspects drive the physical aspects is not an easy task. Trusting the Creator to believe that spiritual aspect of our existence will win the war requires a significant sacrifice. But, I believe that is what God is asking us to do. He has given us the world, the talents that drive us, the fear that leads to knowledge[9], the understanding that provides insight. It isn't physical sacrifice He is seeking, He delights in us[10] and it is our appreciation of what He provides that makes Him happy. That is why He deserves the honor we give Him with our gifts of the first fruits[11]. That is why we worship Him. He is the One that sacrificed for us! He is the One who gave up His son to prove love is more important than substance. He is the One who gives and gives and gives. He is the One who has set the examples. He is the One who gave up a life to prove a spiritual existence takes precedence over a physical life. He is the One who proved life is worth giving, so live THIS Sacrificed Life!

QUESTIONS:

Hope, faith, love and sacrifice are all part of sacrificing to be right with God. But it is a two-sided coin. We have these attributes and most of our thoughts are probably centered around how we are to attend to these attributes with respect to our relationship with God. We might even digress and think about how these attributes need to be expressed with each other. Perhaps, though, maybe it would be more worthwhile to think about how God uses these attributes to relate to us!

1. What challenges do you have when you consider what is involved with the "hope" you have in accepting Jesus' sacrifice for your life?
2. Describe the faith you have when it comes to accepting the sacrifice that Jesus made when he allowed himself to be nailed to the cross.

3. How would you describe God's love for you as expressed with the sacrifice of His son on the cross?

4. How do the physical demands of your existence interfere with your spiritual needs?

5. Describe the physical needs you have and attach some degree of order to them if you can.

6. Describe the spiritual needs you have and attach some degree of order to them if you can.

7. When it comes to making a choice between your physical needs and your spiritual needs, which takes precedent?

8. What aspects of Jesus' ministry can you think of that address your physical needs? Your spiritual needs?

9. How did Jesus' sacrifice of his life on the cross make "things" right for you with God?

References:

1. The Nature of Atonement (Four Views) edited by Beilby and Eddy, InterVarsity Press, 2006

2. 1Corentihiens 13: 8—13

3. Exodus 20:13

4. John 3:16

5. "Adventures with Apples and Snakes In The Garden Of Eden"; George M. Goodrich; Author House; 2010

6. Matthew 20:28

7. Matthew 5: 3 – 13

8. Matthew 5: 21 – 48

9. Proverbs 1: 7

10. Psalm 149: 4

11. Proverbs 3: 9

PRELUDE

WE HAVE THE EXAMPLE, CHRIST saw to that! But now the challenge becomes how do we hone our behavior, so we achieve the desired results? First, I think we need to understand what the desired results truly are. I am in no way going to attempt to describe what God has in mind for anyone to achieve those desired results. However, I do believe we have it in our power to do our best to live up to our individual understanding of what God expects of each one of us. Secondly, I submit we are not clueless of those expectations. All we must do is take stock of our passions and skills and surroundings, all of which are God's gifts to us for our existence. Thirdly, each of us can strive for the best results in anything we endeavor to try. Perfection may not be achieved, but that doesn't mean we shouldn't strive to achieve it!

CHAPTER 17
Sacrifice THIS Perfection

What is it about perfection,
That striving for it can be an infection?

IN MY IMAGINATION, I USED to think God didn't want to include me
in the process of making "things" right between Him and me. I didn't
really understand why I needed an intercessor to speak for me in my
desire to atone for my sins. After all, it was me, my bad self, that acted
to separated me from God. Why couldn't I approach God to find out
what I had to do to make it right with Him? Was it not enough for
me to want to belong to that special Kingdom of right relationships?
It was just hard for me to imagine God wouldn't want me to make
the required effort to belong to this special Kingdom. It wasn't until I
realized that God only existed in perfection and that for Him to accept
me in His presence, a perfect me would be required. It isn't hard to
imagine that I am a long way from perfection and I am a long way
from being able to achieve the necessary perfection without some sort
of intercession. I could be mistaken, but I think maybe, just maybe
somehow Christ has the answer!

In 2004 I was honored to be selected to present the Hoyt Memorial
Lecture for the Annual American Foundry Convention in Rosemont
Illinois. This lecture is the keynote presentation for the annual meeting
of the Society. To be selected to give this lecture for an entire industry
was to say the least, unexpected. It is still difficult for me to accept

that others thought enough of what I thought to ask me to share in a national forum. I guess I could say I definitely wasn't putting my light under a basket. The topic I chose was perfection and the title was "The Absence of Perfection"[1]. Since this was a special honor, I chose the opportunity to technically address the issue of obtaining perfection in the quality of a casting. My 40 year career in metallurgical engineering had been spent doing defect analysis and failure analysis, so I thought it would be appropriate to share what I had learned about the missing issues of perfection that were the cause for the defects and failures.

This perfection issue is worth sharing again in the light of this understanding that God requires perfection in order to be in His presence. Striving for perfection, indeed, is worth every effort and requires some means to determine how successful one is at achieving the desired result. This is a little "tongue in cheek", but just the same, God's idea of perfection could be a little different than our idea. I read a story about Jessica Parks from North Branch, Michigan, relating how she drove a car with her feet because she was born without arms. There was a picture of her backing her car out of the driveway on her way to take a driver's license test[2].

Perfection and success, in some respects are dependent on each other. However, this situation with Jessica Parks makes me wonder if perfection is divided into parts and whether or not we are spoiled because sometimes success can be achieved with only part of perfection.

Perfection also has a certain degree of elusiveness. Most would agree perfection is in the eye of the beholder and a definite function of mind set. Motorcycles are an excellent example; I am a Honda rider, or at least, I used to be until I lost my sense of balance due to an extreme illness. A Harley rider once exclaimed when he examined my bike, "How do you work on that?" (He used a little more colorful language to express his concern than is permitted in a book like this.) To him perfection was being able to fix the bike when something broke. To me, perfection was having a bike that didn't break.

I guess one can say a significant amount of advice exists that tells us how to achieve perfection. My career has been mostly in the failure analysis business. We have many tools that permit us to identify the cause for failures. However, in researching the topic of perfection, I did not find tools that could measure perfection. So, I made up a few with a little help from some friends:

Repeat-o-tometer: This is a device that measures the amount of hair loss resulting from beating your head against the wall to get someone to do it correctly the first time.

Epitomic Caliper: This measures the epitome of perfection.

Pinnacle-imeter: To determine the height of perfection.

Panoram-i-tron: A viewing devise that permits us to see all sides of perfection at the same time.

Silaphone: An instrument to replace the telephone because with infinite perfection, the "tell a phone" will be silent.

Quantifiscope: A viewing device that permits one to observe the magnitude of perfection.

An N-V plotter (as opposed to the X-Y plotter) that permits one to graphically display the envy others have for your perfection.

Of course, these tools are a spoof on perfection, but, they do indicate a perspective that is not associated with the tools used when performing defect analysis or failure analysis.

Many people have provided their insights about perfection. I will share a few observations about some of these insights.

Don't let embarrassment get in the way of asking. "I would rather attempt to do something great and fail than to do nothing and succeed."[3] Although I heard this on one of Dr. Schuler's Sunday morning sermons, it has also been part of my philosophy. "Do something even if it is wrong." It has amazed me during my career that we hardly ever have time to do a job correctly, but we always have time to do it over.

Once perfection is acquired, it can become easier. Here are some interesting statistics for a game where perfection has a definite identity...a 300 game in bowling. In 1952 a total of 198 bowlers had sanctioned 300 games. In 1980, the pinnacle year for the number of ABC league bowlers, 4.8 million, 5,373 perfect games were bowled. By comparison, the 2001-02 season had only 1.7 million ABC league bowlers but they bowled 42,163 perfect games.[4] Of course, one can argue the bowlers didn't get better, the equipment did. Perhaps it was the changes in the equipment that took place in this time period, but human understanding of the game kinetics caused the equipment improvements that resulted in this perfection quest. So, success at perfection is possible, but the rewards change. For example, instead of being given a gold ring for a perfect game like the old timers, now, when a perfect game is bowled, the bowler has the privilege of "buying" a ring.

The point is in God's creation, mankind can achieve perfection, but the perfection God is seeking for his Kingdom is only achievable when sin is absent. We as humans can never achieve the perfection required to be in God's Kingdom simply because our worldly selves have no way to exist without experiencing sin. We simply can not possibly be totally dependent on God for everything. It just is not in our nature. We are raised from the beginning to be independent. We are taught on purpose to fend for ourselves and to rely on out talents, our God given talents, yes, to provide for our needs. Those needs, both physical and spiritual are fulfilled with God's help, but we somehow believe the pleasures that result are our rewards for being the kind of person we believe God wants us to be. How silly! The perfection God wants can only be achieved when we start fresh with an attitude that all we have is from God and God deserves all the glory for what is achieved. Fortunately, God has provided a way to achieve that perfection. "For God so loved the world that he gave his one and only Son, that whoever believes in him shall not perish but have eternal life."[5] God has always required a sacrifice to make up for (atone for) the sins we commit in our "absence of perfection", but unless we accept the sacrifice He made in the life of His son, we can not possibly make a sacrifice that sufficiently satisfies God's requirements for perfection to live in his presence forever. So, sacrifice your concept of perfection and take up God's perfection, Jesus, if you want the privilege of living with God forever as He originally intended when He gave us the gift of free will.

QUESTIONS:

I believe that if one is going to be in the presence of God, no sin, no unrighteous, no hate, no self-promoting individualism of any sort will be tolerated. How we accomplish that is impossible if we were to try to do it ourselves. We will probably spend a life time trying to figure out how to accomplish the task. But God wants us in His presence. To be there requires us to accept the path that Jesus provided. According to him, there is no other way.

1. How do we hone our behavior, so we achieve the desired results as Jesus exemplified?
2. Why is an intercessor necessary to make things right between us and God?
3. If you are going to be in the presence of God, what do you think you need to do before God will let you be in His presence?
4. How do you figure out what God expects of you as an individual?
5. Why do you think God expects you to at least try to be perfect in your efforts to do His will?
6. How do you think your idea of perfection differs from God's idea of perfection?
7. How does the concept of Jesus' death and resurrection meet the requirements of perfection in God's will?
8. What aspects of your life do you believe reflects the perfection that you think God expects?
9. What aspect of your life do you think is as far away from what God expects as perfection as one can get?

REFERENCES:

1. The Absence of Perfection 108th Metal Casting Congress American Foundry Society, paper 04-083

2. South Bend Tribune MI edition Wednesday, May 7, 2003 pg D10 "Remarkable Feet"
3. Hour of Power Broadcast 2003
4. 300 Loses Luster, "USA TODAY" Sports Section Wednesday, December 4, 2002
5. John 3:16

PRELUDE

Understanding how these events in the last week of Jesus' life reflect God's love for his mankind creation is not an easy matter. But then how we think of them reflects our individual life's experiences. Our reactions depend on what we know and what we have learned as we have journeyed through our lives. What we believe becomes the real challenge that only our faith can overcome. Common sense does not apply, but the lessons in love go way beyond what our most active imagination could possible conjure.

CHAPTER 18
Live Up To THIS Love

When everything is said and done
It was Christ that really won!

LIKE ALL GOOD CHRISTIANS, I have accepted Jesus Christ as my personal savior. In fact, one time, I remember a complete stranger asking me if I had accepted Jesus as my personal savior. This occasion occurred as I was filling my gas tank at a filling station. The person was sharing the same pump island but on the opposite side. My response was "yes I had" and then I inquired of the stranger whether or not he had accepted the fact that I had accepted Jesus as my personal savior. He didn't quite know how to respond. That seems to be an issue doesn't it? We all might accept Jesus as our savior, but we don't all accept him the same way. If all of us were to accept Jesus the same way, we wouldn't have a mixture of Catholics, Protestants, Mennonites, Amish, Latter Day Saints, Jehovah Witness, etc., and all the subgroups: Methodist, Baptist, Presbyterian, Seventh Day Adventist, Reformed, Covenant, and many many others. Even within my own congregation, we have individuals that seem to anguish over how we demonstrate our Christianity. All these differences exist just because Christ directed us to love one another as he has loved us[1]. How we interpret what this statement means is different for each of us because we consider the statement from the standpoint of our life experiences. The best interpretation I have encountered is to act in such manner that others can see Christ through us as I said in Chapter 16. None of us have the same life experiences, so we don't have the same "home position" from which to consider this statement to enable others to see Christ through us. By "home position" I mean that state of existence each one of us considers as the platform from which we view life and the surrounding relationships; the platform we can come back too when we get distracted and can count on having a familiar view; the platform is always the same and we can have a fresh start from a position we know and understand.

"Seeing Christ through us" was a response an acquaintance used in one of our study groups when I asked the question about how to do what Christ would do. This question has always challenged me because, I am definitely not Christ and have no basis to be able to completely understand how to do what Christ would do without really wondering if what I would do was what Christ would do or would it be what I think Christ would do. One evening, I had an occasion to see this person arguing vociferously with another member of our congregation. The disagreement was about the wording being used to portray our church's core values. In the middle of one of his loudest arguments, I would like to have asked him if I was seeing Christ through him or was I seeing him. However, I think he recognized his own situation, because he calmed down and proceeded to seek a way of seeing the other side of the argument and to settle on the wording we now have. The disagreement was over the use of the word "compel". Our value statement indicates God's love for us compels us to love God back, love our fellow Christians, love our neighbors, and to love our enemies. So, the sacrifice part that Jesus did during that last week is only part of the story. The sacrifice was a necessary part, but how does it also include God's love?

Even this statement of allowing others to "see Christ through us" leaves much to be desired to have just one umbrella over how we as Christians need to respond to life's constant challenges. I wish I had an answer that would satisfy everyone, but after writing this book I can understand none of us will ever have the same perspective. I can honestly say, however, my understanding of the need for Christ to be hung on the cross has a different perspective than the understanding I had before I started. I still admit, however, seeking the meaning of this sacrificial act has not lost the patina that seems to cover the event and to keep us from coming to a common response that satisfies everyone. I will say I do have a deeper understanding of the magnitude of the love that drove God to sacrifice His own son just to prove His love is eternal.

Jesus told Nicodemus that to see the Kingdom of God one had to be born again[2]. In our wisdom, we have interpreted that to mean we each need to go through a spiritual birth in addition to our physical birth. I believe that is true, but I also believe it is only part of the requirement. Jesus showed us the rest of this requirement when he actually died on the cross and was reborn on the third day. He died for our sins, yes. But that is only part of the reason he was put on the cross. He overcame death just to prove something much more meaningful was at stake, God's love! Our lives are full of rebirth situations, but we probably don't consider them as such. We find we need to "let go" in order to accept situations that are beyond our control. In a sense, we are experiencing a "rebirth" to move on with our lives.

In a family situation, it isn't uncommon for children to think the father's job was lacking in the father/child relationship and it isn't uncommon for the father to think the child could be better than what appears to have been achieved. Most fathers believe their children are the greatest and the father is prouder of the children than the children actually realize. I know that is how I believe. The difficulty is neither the father nor the child really knows how to communicate their feelings without raising the child's suspicious nature and consequently the child considers the father's input as being critical of the child's behavior. The truth of the matter is usually the father is simply trying to give the child the benefit of the father's experience and his desire to be part of the child's life. I can't help but wonder if maybe these issues are the same issues that exist between God and each of us. I think God was and is trying to help us understand just how much He actually loves us using the trials and tribulations that Jesus had to endure to prove that obedience to God is the only way to experience that love.

Think about all the actions that took place in that last week of Jesus' life. Think about those actions from God's perspective: the mouths He created were not kind to His son; they spewed words of hate and probably spewed physical saliva as well. The hands He had created nailed His son to the cross[3]. Imagine if you were God the creator of the universe, would you have come to earth as a person? Would you have put up with the living conditions that required you to be born in a stable, a place where animals lived? Would you have accepted the way those who were "your chosen people" celebrated their self-serving position in the sacraments they use to honor you? Yet, God did come to earth as a person[4] and withstood all these humiliating experiences. Most of all, this personification of God demonstrated the one essential trait that is needed to be in God's kingdom: obedience. Obedience even unto death. As I was writing this book, I realized every one of us at birth has the potential of being a Son of God if only we could be obedient to all of God's commands. From the time we are "potty trained" to our death, we are encouraged to be independent individuals capable of acting for ourselves, thinking for ourselves, sustaining ourselves, and basically existing on our own. Yet, while we are being encouraged to be independent, God is trying his hardest to keep us dependent on and obedient to Him.

God loves His creation[5, 6, & 7] and we are all part of it. He loves His creation so much He gave us His son[8]. Yes, His son was sacrificed for our sins, but that was only part of the reason this gift was given to us. Jesus was born of God to show us how to obey and to show us how to love. Most of us Christians have accepted the savior part and we are working on the love part even though we know loving our enemies is a requirement that is most challenging. We have a long way to go to live up to the obedient part. God created us to have a free will and He has given us many talents along with a world full of interesting challenges that require us to use our talents to exist in the world. We thrive on the challenges we experience. Uncovering the secrets God has left for us to discover, starting with procreation of life itself leaves us excited to experience even more! The elation we experience when we discover something God has given to us that no one else has understood is hard to explain. I think of such mundane things as electric lights, telephones, computers, automobiles, television, airplanes, and a host of other developments that have occurred just in my life time. The consequence is we believe we have an independence that only requires us to call upon God when we get into trouble.

Let me try to use these events from the last week of Jesus' life to view these three attributes (sacrifice, love, and obedience) from a perspective you may not have considered before this. I know what I am going to ask you to do is a difficult task, because of the reverence with which you hold your beliefs about God and your relationship with your savior, God's son Jesus. Just the same, put your imagination to work and think about trading positions with Jesus as he was subjected to all the degrading events that transpired during that last week. If you are anything like me, putting yourself in Jesus' position is way beyond what you think is possible. Just for a moment, try to challenge your righteous self and make believe you are Jesus. Now that you have traded places, try to imagine the tremendous amount of faith Jesus had to have to be so willing to go through all the humiliation he endured in that last week.

In the end you know you are going to be put to death. Your humanness, however, tells you death is final as far as the existence of your body is concerned. You might believe that who you are or what you are isn't the body but is something else outside of the body. The body is just a residing place for the being you really are. What is more, your experience tells you once your body dies, what you are doesn't have a place to exist. Now comes the hard part: do you have enough faith to believe what Jesus believed that after 3 days, what you are will still be? I don't know about you, but that kind of faith is way beyond what I can muster let alone believe. My wife has asked on numerous occasions; what good is faith if you don't use it? The tremendous amount of faith I would require going through the act of allowing myself to be put to death so that I could come back to life 3 days later just to prove God's love and my obedience is still way beyond my understanding. Yet, that is what Jesus did. I have often thought God had a secret. Jesus, His son, knew that secret as well. It was a secret because after all, Jesus hadn't read the New Testament yet! That secret was death isn't the end! We know the secret now as well. I sensed, however, Jesus' actions during that final week indicated he had some reservations about the outcome of this sacrificial act. Jesus' humanness required a huge amount of faith in his Father to believe his temple would be rebuilt three days later[8].

Can you imagine the amount of love that is required to be that obedient? That is the message Jesus wants us to understand. That is the driving force for us to want to transform our lives in such a manner others can see Christ through us.

The challenge is for us to live up to THAT love or looking at it in a different light, live into THAT love!

QUESTIONS:

Now that we have explored the events that occurred in Jesu's life the last week he lived on earth, we need to explore the significance of these events on how we view the lessons he taught us about love, sacrifice, hope, obedience, and faith. Most of all however, we need to put into practice what those lessons have to do with how we obey God's intentions for our lives.

1. Can you describe your acceptance of Jesus Christ as your personal savior in words that others can accept?
2. Would using your denominations description of how you accept Jesus Christ as your personal savior help you with your description?
3. What aspects of your life can you use to attest to your acceptance of Jesus Christ as your personal savior?
4. As you have grown in your understanding of accepting Jesus Christ as your personal savior, how has your life changed?
5. From what you have learned in this book, what is the one essential trait required to exist in God's kingdom?
6. Why did God let His son be born of man and live on earth?

7. What must happen in your life to cause you to call upon God for help?

8. Can you name three attributes that Jesus life taught us during his short time on earth?

9. What was the secret that God and Jesus knew that allowed Jesus to go through with his plan to be sacrificed?

REFERENCES:

1. John 13:34
2. John 3:3
3. "A Love Worth Giving" by Max Lucado 2002, Thomas Nelson, Publisher
4. Matthew 1:23
5. Zephaniah 3:17
6. Psalm 147:11
7. Psalm 149:4
8. John 3:16
9. John 2:19

Printed in the United States
By Bookmasters